Organic Building Materials in Residential Constructions

About the Authors

Dr. Sucheta Singh is Subject Matter Specialist/Assistant Professor (Home Science), Directorate of Extension Education, G.B. Pant University of Agriculture and Technology, Pantnagar, Uttaranchal. Since seven years, she is involved in dissemination of frontier technologies and development of models for upliftment of rural women. She has many awards and honours and about 50 publications to her credit.

Prof. Veena Gandotra is formerly the Head and Dean, Department of Home Management, Faculty of Community Sciences and Family Studies, The Maharaja Sayajirao University of Baroda. She has carried out many research projects in the areas of management, environment, housing and interiors. She has eleven books and several articles to her credit.

Prof. Promila Sharma is Head, Department of Family Resource Management, College of Home Science, G.B. Pant University of Agriculture and Technology, Pantnagar, Uttaranchal. She has been involved in research since 1983 and disseminated several technologies/techniques through extension and research work.

Organic Building Materials in Residential Constructions

Dr. Sucheta Singh
Assistant Professor/Subject Matter Specialist
Directorate of Extension Education
G.B.Pant University of Agiculture and Technology
Pantnagar, U.S. Nagar-263145, Uttaranchal, India.

Dr. Veena Gandotra
Retired Professor and Dean
Home Management Department
The Maharaja Sayajirao University of Baroda
Vadodara-390002, Gujarat, India.

Dr. Promila Sharma
Professor and Head
Department of Family Resource Management
College of Home Science
G.B.Pant University of Agiculture and Technology
Pantnagar, U.S. Nagar-263145, Uttaranchal, India.

CONCEPT PUBLISHING COMPANY, NEW DELHI-110059

ISBN-13: 978-81-8069-632-9 **ISBN-10: 81-8069-632-4**

First Published 2009

Published and Printed by

Concept
Since 1974

Concept Publishing Company

Regd. Office:

A/15-16, Commercial Block, Mohan Garden

New Delhi-110059 (India)

Phones: 25351460, 25351794, *Fax*: 091-11-25357109

Email: publishing@conceptpub.com,

website: www.conceptpub.com

Editorial Office:

H-13, Bali Nagar, New Delhi-110 015, India.

Cataloging in Publication Data--*Courtesy:* D.K. Agencies (P) Ltd. <docinfo@dkagencies.com>

Singh, Sucheta.

Organic building materials in residential constructions / Sucheta Singh, Veena Gandotra, Promila Sharma.

p. cm.

Study conducted in Nainital District from hill areas and Udham Singh Nagar District from plain areas of Uttarakhand, India.

Includes bibliographical references and index (p.).

ISBN 13: 9788180696329 ISBN 10: 8180696324

1. Building materials--Environmental aspects--India--Naini Tal (District) 2. Building materials--Environmental aspects--India--Udham Singh Nagar (District) 3. House construction--Environmental aspects--India--Naini Tal (District) 4. House construction--Environmental aspects--India--Udham Singh Nagar (District) 5. Organic architecture--India--Naini Tal (District) 6. Organic architecture--India--Udham Singh Nagar (District) 7. Housing and health--India--Naini Tal (District) 8. Housing and health--India--Udham Singh Nagar (District) I. Gandotra, Veena, joint author. II. Sharma, Promila, 1955-, joint author. III. Title.

DDC 720.47095451 22

Dr. B.S. Bisht
Vice-Chancellor

G.B. Pant University
of Agriculture & Technology
PANTNAGAR-263145
Distt. Udham Singh Nagar (Uttarakhand)
INDIA

Dated : November 29, 2008

Foreword

Impact of building materials on indoor environment and health of families is far from organized and comprehensive. An attempt has been made to bring such information in a comprehensive compilation in the form of book entitled "Organic Building Materials in Residential Constructions." It is a step towards sensitizing all concerned about the building materials, psychological and physiological well being of the human beings and quality of indoor environment.

A unique feature of this book is that special attention has been given to organic building materials and their effect on psychological well being of residents. This really needs focus in order to harness relationship among organic building materials, housing conditions and health of the residents.

I compliment Dr. Sucheta Singh, Prof. Veena-Gandotra and Prof. Promila Sharma for their effort in publication of this important book. I am sure that the scientific information contained in the form of various chapters on different aspects will be useful for the planners, policy makers, researchers and all those who are engaged in the construction and occupation of building construction. The valuable information in the book can also be used as a reference for students at graduate and post graduate level as well as scientists and executives.

(B.S. Bisht)
Vice-Chancellor

Preface

A stage of saturation has long passed in many countries in exploitation of environment. However, in India, people are reversing back to nature. They have started practicing organic agriculture, herbal products, eco-friendly products, sustainable environment, etc.

The emphasis today, world-wide, is on organic products. Eco-friendly materials such as wood, clay, thatch, stone, etc. have been used long back to construct homes. Now a days many other natural as well as man-made organic building materials (OBM) are being used. Organic materials are perhaps the oldest construction materials but recently they have been noticed by scientists and researchers. Through many generations of use, people have found ways of getting around some of the limitations of natural organic construction materials.

Human performance is dynamic and is affected by various personal, demographic as well as environmental factors. Although many efforts have been done to find out effect of housing in terms of temperature, relative humidity, age of building structure, years of occupancy, gender, dampness, etc. it is not very much easy to conclude or draw pictures of the association between poor health and housing.

In this context an exploratory study on organic building materials used in residential constructions has been conducted. Major emphasis of this investigation is on bringing forth major issues regarding organic building materials, their availability and extent of use, knowledge about OBM, satisfaction, effects on health, and effect of the indoor environment on the residents.

This book entails a need to understand the impact of building materials on indoor environment and health of families. It attempts to describe issues related with Organic Building Materials, environmental factors affecting indoor housing conditions, health problems due to indoor environment in residential buildings, identification of defective symptoms/deterioration in residential constructions and remedial measures to safeguard OBM and measures to control indoor problems in residential constructions.

Sucheta Singh
Veena Gandotra
Promila Sharma

Contents

1 Introduction

> *"Home is where the heart can laugh without shyness. Home is where the heart's tears can dry at their own pace".*
>
> (Baker, 2005)

It is a well-established fact that grasses and foliages remove carbondioxide from the atmosphere and act like a body of water to reduce the heat. Replacement with building materials, on the other hand, breaks this cycle and creates a hot air barrier that blocks the normal flow of winds and rains.

Earlier eco-friendly materials such as wood, clay, stones, mud, etc. have been used in construction of residential buildings (Taylor, 2000). Natural polymers such as bitumen sealants in construction activities were used for water proofing in the ancient cities of Harappa, Mohenjodaro, Lothal etc. However, buildings created since the 1950s contained plastics in applications such as piping, windows, roofing, flooring, cable sheathing, ducting and insulation (Verma, 2003).

Organic Building Materials and Housing

Organic materials are perhaps the oldest construction materials (Merritt, 1986) but recently they have been noticed by scientists and researchers. Through many generations of use, people have found ways of getting around some of the limitations of natural organic construction materials. Organic building materials are engineering materials which are mixture of different hydrocarbons sometimes together with sulphur, nitrogen and oxygen derivatives, used in residential constructions. (Raghavan, 1996)

Wood is a versatile and widely used structural engineering material for indoor and outdoor applications (Pandey, 2003). Use of wood in building construction and decoration is still considered of higher aesthetic value than other competing materials. Depleting forests leading to rising prices has only made alternative materials more competitive but has not taken the shine off wood (Jain and Mehta, 2003).

Polymers are organic substances and derivatives of carbon and hydrogen. They are also known as 'plastics' (Agrawal, 1988). PVC, PTFE, Polyehylene are widely used organic polymers in building industry (Raghavan, 1998).

Rubbers are highly elastic and resilient polymeric materials which find wide applications in various fields. They are organic polymers that are capable of being subjected to large elastic strains without plastic yielding (Agrawal, 1988). Sponge rubber is used in sealing, heat insulating, cushioning and shock absorptions in buildings (Sastry et al., 1998).

Bitumen is a primary engineering material functioning as a binder in buildings and roads. It acts as a weather proofing membrane in roofing and structural applications. Its thermoplastic nature, water resistance and adhesion towards most other substances make it unique as a building material (Khursheed et al., 2003).

Glues obtained from animal gelatins, vegetables and starches are widely used adhesives. Adhesives made from polymers include cellulose acetate, cellulose acetate butyrates and pyroxylin. Xanthan gum is commercially the most widely produced gum (Sastry, 1998).

Thus, organic building materials have been used from earlier days but they have been modified and protected by use of new organic substances such as plastics, rubber and other materials.

Organic Building Materials and Effects of Environment

The process of weathering is defined as the action of

atmospheric elements in altering the colour, texture, composition or form of exposed objects, ultimately leading to disintegration or failure to perform a function. The well-known elements of weather are radiation, moisture, thermal conditions and gases (Vadstrup, 2005).

Due to long-term exposure for humidity, sooner or later the decay has reached a critical limit for the service life of the materials. The decay of wood due to natural exposure is more or less predictable. Another reason for long service life of wood is the "favourable" climate (a combination of generally low precipitation and low temperature) and constructions based on long-term experience. At the same time, expanding use of surface treatment by tar products, oil paint, linseed-oil paint and stains gave further protection from humidity and prolonged the service life. "Unpredicted" or extensive decay is often due to relatively clear events/ change in exposure.

Norwegian studies by Mattson and Oftedal in 2005 indicated quite clearly that the decay of wood due to natural exposure is more or less predictable. One explanation is the traditionally use of pine logs with an extensive amount of heartwood, which ensure a clear linitation regarding to growth of wood-decaying fungi and wood-boring insects.

The environmental factors collated by following five causes are responsible for most of the deterioration and damages in the organic building materials (Vadstrup, 2005):

1. *Influence of Water*: and the consequences or followers of water (moisture, ice, saltwater, acid rain): This causes dry rot and fungus in wood, salts in masonry and stones, frost damages, acid deterioration, algae, dirt etc.
2. *Mechanical Causes:* from wear, ground decreases, insufficient carrying capacity and wind.
3. *Technical Faults:* from insufficient constructions, leakages, insufficient adjoints between materials, too

hard and moisture tight surface treatments or finishing coats, changes in the physical balance in the constructions.

4. *Forced Deterioration*: of the surface materials due to leakages in the roof, joints, watertight surface on iron etc.
5. *Other Causes:* incorrect use and arrangements, neglect of maintenance.

Thus, changed use (no more heating, lack of maintenance) or construction of the buildings (new materials, thermal insulation) may be the factors that provoke an accelerated rate of decay. Even small changes, such as applying a modern paint system, can be sufficient for a major change in rate of decay.

Housing and Health

Housing conditions are associated with health status in a variety of ways (Townsend et al., 1988). People complain that they become sick in buildings of poor insulation, energy conservation and ventilation with symptoms of eye, throat and nose irritation, dryness of mucosa of skin, erythema and mental fatigue. Displeasures are also experienced with aversive and persistent odours and with ventilation noise (Ahlstrom *et al.* 1986 and Andersen *et al.*, 1975).

Problems of sick buildings concern exposure to irritating agents in indoor air. They may affect the olfactory system, the trigeminal system, the cutaneous system as well as cognitive functions (Bergland *et al.*, 1986).

Sick buildings subject the inhabitants to air which is polluted by mould spores and mould metabolites, volatile hydrocarbons, radon, asbestos particles or other agents. The reactions to air borne chemical compounds and aerosols lead to itchy eyes, dry mucous membranes, abnormal fatigue, headache, or other psychosomatic reactions (Ryd, 1991).

Damp conditions particularly condensation encourage the growth of mould. Mould is less likely to be found in conditions of penetrating or rising damp since the salts which emerge with the moisture tend to inhibit its growth. Condensation on the other hand, contains relatively pure water which is highly conducive to the growth and proliferation of fungal spores, which live off the organic material on walls and in cavities. Fungal spores can give rise to three types of reactions; allergies, infections and toxic effects (Hunt, 1993).

The housing conditions thus have a definite impact on health of the people living in it and make a place where one seeks refuge from the anxieties and worries of the outside world.

Health and Human Behaviour

Biological status can influence psychological state, but psychological status cannot affect biological status (Keithley, 1993). It is growing awareness of the importance of individual behaviour in determining the patterns of health and disease in the population which represents perhaps the greatest single change affecting public health in recent years (Public Health in England, HMSO, 1988).

The cost of living in sick buildings is much higher than accepted if you count the psychological effects. This is more pronounced if sick building is your home. The concepts which should be studied and are studied by different people, in order to show the importance of building 'healthy homes' are:

1. Cognition,
2. Belongingness and identification,
3. Feelings, devotion and love,
4. Memories,
5. Sexual behaviour and social association,

6. Unity and order,
7. Self-identity and gender differences,
8. Privacy, refuge and security,
9. Social and family relationship.

(Ryd, 1991).

Bergland *et al.* in 1987 designed to study sick building syndrome with a battery of diverse psychological tests (reaction time, short-term memory, vigilance, and steadiness) to assess human performance. The trends were found in the expected direction. Memory is considered central to all cognitive functions and it was tested with a commonly used short-term memory task (Peterson *et al.*, 1959).

Housing conditions not only have impact on physical well-being but also mental well-being of the people as reported by various researchers.

Rationale for the Study

> *"Social Science should not be seen as developing a stock of knowledge about an object which is external to us, but should develop a critical self-awareness in people or subjects and indeed assist in their emancipation."*

(Sayer, 1984)

Building materials are most important materials for human beings. Wood, a renewable resource is most abundantly and naturally occurring organic polymeric composite material which consists of long cellulosic fibres (Sastry *et al.*, 2003). In India, the estimated demand of timber is 56.98 million cubic meter in the year 2001-2006. Limitation of plywood/timber in terms of reuse value could be effectively mitigated by the use of new polymeric materials (Singh and Gupta, 2003). Organic polymers are becoming day by day important due to their binding and insulation characteristics (Chand, 2003). Currently about 3.7 million tones of plastics are produced in India for different uses. Their consumption as building material is close to 1.35 m tones. By 2006-07, the production of plastics is expected to reach about 8 million tones in which the share of plastic for building is about 2.4 million tones (Singh & Gupta, 2003).

> *"Home means refuge and security, a place to which we turn to replenish our energies. What does it mean to us if we feel threats against our health in the very place where we need to feel comfortable and at ease?"*
>
> (Ryd, 1991)

In Uttaranchal, the spatial organization of a typical house is rather simple, functional and linear. Timber is used in conjunction with brick or stonewalls to create a composite structure. A wooden frame of joists and columns is made to support the building. Other building materials predominantly used for the construction purposes are composites of organic and inorganic materials, synthetic polymers or plastics, finished stones, marbles, etc. Typologically, in the urban *pols* they are deep wall-to-wall houses with a narrow frontage that opens onto a street. The houses create a dense built environment, as each narrow plot is 100 per cent built up as a result of which a sense of security gets developed. It is basically a deep house-plan with three or four sequential room one behind the other. There is typically a small courtyard in the center that brings in light and ventilation. Basements are used for storage and water collection and also for passive cooling in the hot summer months. The optimized and ornate courtyard at the center is an important socio-cultural as well as existential space as a center of household activities. The wooden facades, a dominating element of the house form, have an intricate ordering mechanism, articulated elements and profuse carvings. They are often an expression of the socio-economic status of the owners. The aesthetic vocabulary of making is created with horizontal bands and vertical fenestrations. There is composite construction in brick and wood. At times, burnt brick was used with mud mortar. Wooden structure is evolved through the beam and joist system with made-up floors. The internal courtyard is also a spatial aesthetic experience with the woodwork contributing a great deal. The finely carved columns, brackets and balconies are predominant elements.

The state has declared itself as an organic state. People are carefully choosing to produce organic foods and fibres to feed and clothe their families, but they should not forget to regard the construction and furnishing of their home by the same standards. Deterioration of building materials due to exposure of environmental conditions is more or less unpredictable, which affect indoor housing environment. Housing conditions are among the primary determinants of an individual's health (Foster, 1992; Ineichen, 1993; Krieger, 2002; Xavier *et al.*, 2003). There is a substantial body of evidence on the health impacts (Fuller *et al.*, 2000; Braubach *et al.*, 2001; Ranson 1991; Xavier *et al.*, 2003) and human behaviour (Berglund *et al.*, 1986; Ryd, 1991) due to the housing environment. An increased number of bad houses and an accelerated deterioration of housing stock are on an increase (UNECE, 2002; Hunger, 1994).

There is a less or negligible documentation about the relationship among organic building materials (OBM), housing conditions in OBM houses, health and human behaviour. In home management we are very much concerned with housing for family living. The quality of housing can enhance or diminish the well-being of individual and families as that of the entire community. There is a need to understand the impact of building materials on indoor environment and health of families. Therefore, a need was felt to conduct a study on residences made from organic building materials in order to search a link of the residences with environmental and psychological health issues.

Objectives

1. To make an inventory of Organic Building Materials (OBM) available and their use in residential constructions.
2. To find out extent of use of OBM in residential constructions.
3. To assess problems experienced in care and maintenance in the selected residential constructions.
4. To find out the health problems perceived by the residents due to use of OBM.
5. To ascertain the knowledge and satisfaction level of residents regarding OBM.
6. To assess level of human performance in the selected residential buildings with OBM constructions.
7. To develop an educational material on increasing awareness regarding proper use of OBM.

Delimitations

1. The study will be limited to two districts of Uttaranchal, namely :
   (a) Nainital,
   (b) Udham Singh Nagar.
2. The study will be limited to 200 residents comprising 100 residents in each district.
3. The experiment will be limited to assess :
   (a) Human performance (memory, attentions and mental fatigue),
   (b) Indoor environment (temperature and humidity).

Hypotheses

H_1 : Knowledge regarding OBM, extent of use of OBM in home and problems faced in care and maintenance are associated with personal variables, family variables and situational variables.

H_2 : There is an inter-relationship among knowledge regarding OBM, extent of use of OBM in home and problems faced in its care and maintenance.

H_3 : Knowledge regarding OBM, extent of use of OBM in home and problems faced in care and mainte-nance of the houses are associated with satisfaction derived from use of OBM and effect on health of the residents.

H_4 : Satisfaction derived from use of OBM and effect on health of the residents has an association with personal variables, family variables and situational variables.

H_5 : Temperature and humidity inside the home is associated with extent of use of OBM in the residential constructions.

H_6 : Human performance in terms of short-term memory, attention/concentration and work and fatigue has an association with temperature and humidity inside the home.

Assumption

A variety of organic building materials are used in residential constructions.

2 Review of Literature

There is an abundant amount of literature available on building materials used in masonry, framework, main structure, furnishings, upholsteries, etc. In this chapter literature which is most relevant, contemporary and applicable has been summarized under following heads:

2.1 Organic building materials,
2.2 Environmental factors affecting indoor housing conditions.
2.3 Review of studies in India and abroad:
  (a) Organic building materials,
  (b) Housing and human performance.

2.1 Theoretical Review on Organic Building Materials

A brief description of organic building materials used in building construction on the basis of various studies quoted by Dietz, Harper, Detroit, Wood Handbook by U.S. Government, Modern Plastic Encyclopedia cited in Merrit; 1986, is given below:

(a) Wood

Wood is a natural polymer composed of cells in the shape of long thin tubes with tapered ends. The cell wall consists of crystalline cellulose aligned parallel to the axis of the cell. Typical natural cellulose has several thousands $C_6H_{10}O_5$ molecular units in each chain. The cellulose crystals are bonded together by a complex amorphous lignin composed of carbohydrate compounds. Wood substances are 50 to 60 per cent cellulose and 20 to 35 per cent lignin, the remainder being other carbohydrates and mineral matter. There are different varieties of wood used in construction (Plate-1)

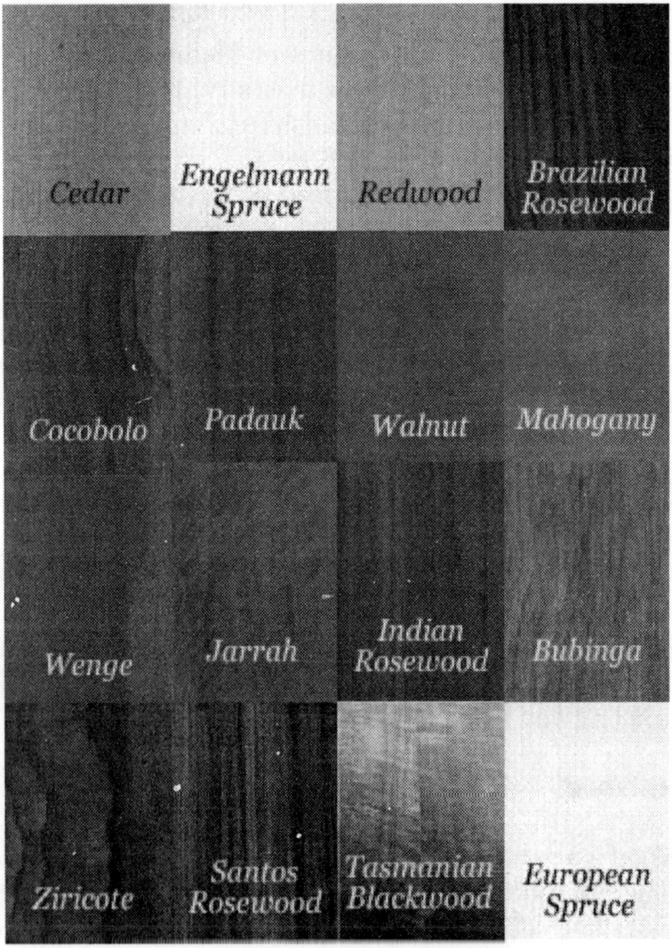

Plate 2.1 : Types of wood used in building constructions

(i) Types of Wood

Diffuse-porous Wood

Certain hard woods in which the pores tend to be uniformly sized and distributed throughout each annual ring or to decrease in size slightly and gradually toward the outer border of the ring.

Early Wood

Portion of the annual growth ring that is formed during the early part of the growing season; it is usually less dense and mechanically weaker than late wood.

Hard Wood

General botanical group of trees that has broad leaves in contrast to the conifers or soft wood.

Late Wood

Portion of the annual growth ring that is formed after the early wood formation has ceased; it is usually denser and mechanically stronger than early wood.

Lumber

Product of the saw and planing mill manufactured from a log through the process of sawing, resawing to width, passing length-wise through a standard planing machine, and crosscutting to length.

Ring-porous Woods

Group of hardwoods in which the pores are comparatively large at the beginning of each annual ring and decrease in size more or less abruptly toward the outer portion of the ring, thus forming a distinct inner zone of pores, the early-wood, and an outer zone with smaller pores, the latewood.

Soft Wood

General botanical group of trees that in most cases has needle like or scale like leaves (the conifers); term has no reference to the actual hardness of the wood. Wood is an extremely versatile material with a wide range of physical and mechanical properties among the many species of wood. It is also a renewable resource with an exceptional strength-to-weight ratio. Wood is a desirable construction material because the energy requirements of wood for producing a usable end-product are much lower than those of competitive materials, such as steel, concrete, or plastic.

(ii) Structure of Wood

The anatomical structure of wood affects strength properties, appearance, resistance to penetration by water and chemicals, resistance to decay, pulp quality, and the chemical reactivity of wood. To use wood most effectively requires knowledge of not only the amounts of various substances that make up wood, but also how those substances are distributed in the cell walls. Woods are either hardwoods or softwoods. Hardwood trees (angiosperms, i.e., plants with covered seeds) generally have broad leaves, are deciduous in the temperate regions of the world, and are porous, i.e., they contain vessel elements. Softwood trees (conifers or gymnosperm, i.e., plants with naked seeds) are cone bearing, generally have scale like or needle like leaves, and are non-porous, i.e., they do not contain vessel elements. The terms hardwood and softwood have no direct relation to the hardness or softness of the wood. In fact, hardwood trees such as cottonwood, aspen, and balsa have softer wood than the western white pines and truc firs; certain softwoods, such as longleaf pine and Douglas-fir, produce wood that is much harder than that of basswood or yellow-poplar. Many mechanical properties of wood, such as bending and crushing strength and hardness, depend upon the density of wood; denser woods are generally stronger. Wood density is determined largely by the relative thickness of the cell wall and by the proportions of thick-walled and thin-walled cells present. The cells that make up the structural elements of wood are of various sizes and shapes and are firmly bonded together. Dry wood cells may be empty or partly filled with deposits such as gums, resins, or other extraneous substances. Long and pointed cells, known as fibres or tracheids, vary greatly in length within a tree and from species to species. Hardwood fibres are –1 mm long, and softwood fibres are -3 to 8 mm. Just under the bark of a tree is a thin layer of cells, not visible to the naked eye, called the cambium. Here, cells divide and eventually differentiate to form bark tissue outside of the cambium and wood or xylem tissue inside of the cambium. This newly formed wood on the inside contains many living cells and conducts sap upward in the tree, and hence, is called sapwood. Eventually, the inner sapwood cells become inactive and are transformed into heartwood. This transformation is often accompanied by the formation of extractives that darken the wood, make it less porous, and sometimes provide more resistance to decay. Because of the great structural variations in wood, there are many possibilities for selecting a species for a specific purpose. Some species, like spruce, combine light weight with relatively high values for stiffness and bending strength. Very heavy woods, like lignum vitae, are extremely hard and resistant to abrasion. A very light wood, like balsa, has high thermal insulation value. Hickory has extremely high shock resistance. Mahogany has excellent dimensional stability.

(iii) Wood Properties

Physical Properties

Physical properties are the quantitative characteristics of wood and its behaviour to external influences other than applied forces. Included here are directional properties, moisture content, dimensional stability, thermal and pyrolytic (fire) properties, density, and electrical, chemical, and decay resistance. Familiarity with physical properties is important because they can significantly influence the performance and strength of wood used in structural applications. The physical properties of wood most relevant to structural design and performance are discussed in this section.

Dimensional Stability

Above the fibre saturation point, wood will not shrink or swell from changes in moisture content because free water is found only in the cell cavity and is not associated within the cell walls. However, wood changes in dimension as moisture content varies below the fibre saturation point. Wood shrinks as it loses moisture below the fibre saturation point and swells as it gains moisture up to the fibre saturation point. These dimensional changes may result in splitting, checking, and warping. The phenomena of dimensional stability and EMC must be understood, Dimensional stability of wood is one of the few properties that significantly differs in each of the three axis directions. Dimensional changes in the longitudinal direction between the fibre saturation point and oven dry are between 0.1 and 0.2 per cent and are of no practical significance; however, in reaction or juvenile wood, these percentages may be significantly higher. The combined effects of shrinkage in the tangential and radial axes can distort the shape of wood pieces because of the difference in shrinkage and the curvature of the annual rings. Generally, tangential shrinkage (varying from 4.4 to 7.8% depending on species) is twice that of radial shrinkage (from 2.2 to 5.6%).

Thermal Expansion

Thermal expansion of dry wood is positive in all directions;

wood expands when heated and contracts when cooled. Wood that contains moisture reacts to temperature changes differently than dry wood. The linear expansion coefficients of dry wood parallel to grain are generally independent of specific gravity and species and range from approximately 3×10^{-6} to 4.5×10^{-6} per °C. The linear expansion coefficients across the grain (tangential and radial) are in proportion to density and range from approximately 5 to 10 times greater than parallel to grain coefficients. When moist wood is heated, it tends to expand because of normal thermal expansion and shrink because of moisture loss from increased temperature. Unless the initial moisture content of the wood is very low (3 to 4%), the net dimensional change on heating is negative. Wood at intermediate moisture contents of approximately 8 to 20 per cent will expand when first heated, then gradually shrink to a volume smaller than the initial volume as moisture is lost in the heated condition.

Electrical Resistance

Wood is a good electrical insulator. However, significant variations in conductivity do exist. These variations in electrical resistance can be related to variations in grain orientation, temperature, and moisture content. The conductivity of wood in the longitudinal axis is approximately twice that in the radial or tangential axis. The electrical conductivity of wood generally doubles for each 10 °C increase in temperature. Generally, variations in conductivity related to wood density and species are considered minor. The correlation between electrical resistivity and moisture content is the basis for electrical resistance type moisture meters that estimate moisture content by measuring the resistance of the wood between two electrodes. Moisture content meters, as these instruments are commonly called, need to be calibrated for temperature and species and are effective only for moisture content ranges of 5 to 25 per cent. They are generally unreliable for high resistivities at moisture contents below 5 or 6 per cent, for estimating the moisture content of green timber, or for estimating moisture content of treated timbers (most treatments alter conductivity).

Decay Resistance

Wood decay fungi and wood-destroying organisms require oxygen, appropriate temperature, moisture, and a food source. Wood will not decay if kept dry (moisture content less than 20%). On the other extreme, if continuously submerged in water at sufficient depths, wood will usually not decay. Whenever wood is intermediary to either of these two extremes, problems with wood decay can result. To avoid problems with decay where moisture cannot be controlled, the engineer or designer can use either naturally durable species or treated timber. The natural durability of wood to the mechanisms and processes of deterioration is related to the anatomical characteristics and species of wood. In general, the outer zone or sapwood of all species has little resistance to deterioration and fails rapidly in adverse environments. For heartwood, natural durability depends on species. Heartwood forms as the living sapwood cells gradually die. In some species, the sugars present in the cells are converted to highly toxic extractives that are deposited in the wood cell wall. Many species produce durable heartwood, including western red cedar, redwood, and black locust; however, durability varies within a tree and between trees of a given species. To enhance durability, wood can be treated with an EPA-registered, toxic preservative chemical treatment.

Chemical Resistance

Wood is highly resistant to many chemicals, which gives it a significant advantage over many alternative building materials. Wood is often considered superior to alternative materials, such as concrete and steel, partly because of its resistance to mild acids (pH more than 2.0), acidic salt solutions, and corrosive agents. Generally, iron holds up better on exposure to alkaline solution than does wood, but wood can be treated with many of the common wood preservatives (e. g., creosote) to greatly enhance its performance in this respect.

Heartwood is far more durable than sapwood to chemical attack because heartwood is more resistant to penetration by liquids. Many preservative treatments, such as creosote or pentachlorophenol in heavy oil, can also significantly increase the ability of wood to resist liquid or chemical penetration, or both. Chemical solutions may induce two general types of action: normal reversible swelling by a liquid and irreversible chemical degradation. With the former, removal of the liquid will return wood to its original condition. With the latter, permanent changes occur within the wood structure from hydrolysis, oxidation, or delignification.

Mechanical Properties

Mechanical properties are the characteristics of a material in response to externally applied forces. They include elastic properties, which characterize resistance to deformation and distortion, and strength properties, which characterize resistance to applied loads. Mechanical property values are given in terms of stress (force per unit area) and strain (deformation resulting from the applied stress). The mechanical property values of wood are obtained from laboratory tests of lumber of straight-grained clear wood samples (without natural defects that would reduce strength, such as knots, checks, splits, etc.).

Shear

When used as a beam, wood is exposed to compression stress on one surface of the beam and tensile stress on the other.

This opposition of stress results in a shearing action through the section of the beam. This parallel-to-grain shearing action is termed horizontal shear. The horizontal shear strength of clear Douglas-fir and loblolly pine averages 6.2 and 5.9 MPa, respectively. Conversely, when stress is applied perpendicular to the cell length in a plane parallel to grain, this action is termed rolling shear. Rolling shear stresses produce a tendency for the wood cells to roll over one another. In general, rolling shear strength values for clear specimens average 18 to 28 per cent of the parallel-to-grain shear values.

Energy Absorption Resistance

Energy absorption or shock resistance is a function of the ability of a material to quickly absorb and then dissipate energy via deformation. Wood is remarkably resilient in this respect and is often a preferred material for shock loading. Several parameters are used to describe energy absorption depending on the eventual criteria of failure considered. Work to proportional limit, work to maximum load, and work to total failure (i. e., toughness) describe the energy absorption of wood materials at progressively more severe failure criteria.

Fatigue

The fatigue resistance of wood is sometimes an important consideration. Wood, like many fibrous materials, is quite resistant to fatigue (i. e., the effects of repeated loading). In many crystalline metals, repeated loadings of 1 to 10 million cycles at stress levels of 10 to 15 per cent of ultimate can induce fatigue type failures. At comparable stress levels, the fatigue strength of wood is often several times that of most metals.

Hardness

Hardness represents the resistance of wood to indentation

and marring. Hardness is comparatively measured by force required to embed a 11.3 mm ball one-half its diameter into the wood.

Environmental Properties

Moisture Content

Mechanical property values of wood increase as wood dries from the fiber saturation point to 10 to 15 per cent moisture content. For clear wood, mechanical property values continue to increase as wood dries below 10 to 15 per cent moisture content. For lumber, studies have shown that mechanical property values reach a maximum at about 10 to 15 per cent moisture content. Then begin to decrease with decreasing moisture content below 10 to 15 per cent. For either product, the effects of moisture content are considered to be reversible in the absence of decay.

Temperature

Strength and stiffness decrease when wood is heated and increase when cooled. The temperature effect is immediate and, for the most part, reversible for short heating durations. However, if wood is exposed to elevated temperatures for an extended time, strength is permanently reduced because of wood substance degradation and a corresponding loss in weight. The magnitude of these permanent effects depends on moisture content, heating medium, temperature, exposure period, and to a lesser extent, species and specimen size. As a general rule, wood should not be exposed to temperatures above 65°C. The immediate effect of temperature interacts with the effect of moisture content so that neither effect can be completely understood without consideration of the other.

Decay and Insect Damage

Wood is conducive to decay and insect damage in moist,

warm conditions. Decay within a structure cannot be tolerated because strength is rapidly reduced in even the early stages of decay. It has been estimated that a 5 per cent weight loss from decay can result in strength losses as high as 50 per cent. If the warm, moist conditions required for decay cannot be controlled, then the use of naturally decay resistant wood species or chemical treatments are required to impede decay. Insects, such as termites and certain types of beetles, can be just as damaging to mechanical performance. Insect infestation can be controlled *via* mechanical barriers, naturally durable species, or chemical treatments.

Reaction to Heat and Fire

The physical and chemical properties of wood, like those of any organic material, are subject to deterioration. The rate and extent of deterioration are governed by the interdependent factors of temperature, time, and moisture. In locations not conducive to decay or insect attack, wood is extremely stable at ordinary temperatures. However, with increasing temperature, the degradation of surface layers progresses into the interior layers. Prolonged heating at temperatures as low as 90 °C may cause charring. In general, the thermal degradation of wood and other cellulosic substances proceed along one of two competing reaction pathways. At temperatures up to –200 °C, carbon-dioxide and traces of organic compounds are formed, in addition to the release of water vapour. The gases are not readily ignitable, but under certain conditions, a pilot flame can ignite the volatiles after 14 to 30 min at 10 °C. Exothermic reactions may occur near 200°C and, in situations where heat is conserved, self-ignition at temperatures as low as 100 °C has been observed. Times and temperatures that might result in smoldering initiation can be determined. To provide a margin of safety, 77 °C should be the upper limit in prolonged exposure near heating devices. Temperatures in excess of 200 °C lead to much more rapid decom-position. Under these conditions, the pyrolysis gases contain 200 or more different components and the degradation is accompanied by reduction in weight, depending on temperature and duration of heating. Thermo-gravimetric analysis of wood [a -cellulose and lignin] indicates that a slow initial weight loss for lignin and wood begins at –200 °C. Differential thermal analyses (delta) of wood and its components indicate that the thermal degradation reactions in an inert atmosphere release less than 5 per cent of the heat released during combustion in air.

Wood in its untreated form has good resistance or endurance to fire penetration when used in thick sections for walls, doors, floors, ceilings, beams, and fire retardant chemicals, such as ammonium phosphate, ammonium sulfate, zinc chloride, guanylurea phosphate, dicyandia-mide phosphate, borax, and boric acid, are often used in combinations. Borax and boric acid mixtures are moderately effective in reducing flamespread and afterglow without premature charring during severe drying operations. Although very hydroscopic, zinc chloride is an effective flame retardant; boric acid is often added to retard afterglow. Fire retardant treatments can adversely affect the strength properties of wood. Elevated temperatures in service can cause further strength loss. Fire retardants such as ammonium sulfate can have a corrosive effect on metal fasteners. In exterior applications, a treatment with resistance to weathering and leaching is important. Solutions of these fire retardant formulations are impregnated into wood under full cell pressure treatment to obtain dry chemical retentions of 65 to 95 kg/m^3; this type of treatment greatly reduces flame-spread and afterglow. These effects are the result of changed thermal decomposition reactions that favour production of carbondioxide and water (vapour) as opposed to more flammable components. Char oxidation (glowing or smoldering) is also inhibited. Some of the chemicals mentioned above and others, such as chlorinated rubber or paraffin, antimony trioxide, calcium carbonate, calcium borate, pentaerythrithol, alumina trihydrate, titanium dioxide, and urea-melamine formaldehyde resin, may be used to formulate fire retardant coatings. Many of these coatings are formulated in such a way that the films intumesce (expand) when exposed to fire, thus insulating the wood surface from further thermal exposure. Fire retardant coatings are mostly used for existing construction.

Resistance to Chemicals

Different species of wood vary in their resistance to chemical attack. The significant properties are believed to be inherent to the wood structure, which governs the rate of ingress of the chemical and the composition of the cell wall, which affects the rate of action at the point of contact. Wood is widely used as a structural material in the chemical industry because it is resistant to a large variety of chemicals. Its resistance to mild acids is far superior to that of steel but not as good as some of the more expensive acid-resistant alloys. Wood tanks used to store cold, dilute acid have a relatively long service life. However, increasing concentration or temperature causes the wood tank to deteriorate rapidly. Softwoods are generally more resistant to acids than are hardwoods because they have high lignin and low hemicellulose contents. In general, heartwood is more resistant to acids than sapwood, probably because of heartwood's higher extractive content and slower movement of liquid into the heartwood. For these reasons, the heartwood of certain conifers has been widely used in the chemical industry. Oxidizing acids, such as nitric acid, attack wood faster than common mineral acids, although wood is frequently used in contact with dilute nitric acid. Oxidizing acids not only attack wood by hydrolysis of the polysaccharides but also degrade these polymers through oxidative reaction. Wood shows excellent resistance to organic acids, which gives it a distinct advantage compared with steel, concrete, rubber, and some plastics. Mild organic acids such as acetic acid have little effect on wood strength.

Alkaline solutions attack wood more rapidly than acids of equivalent concentrations, whereas strong oxidizing chemicals are harmful. Wood is seldom used where resistance to chlorine and hypochlorite solutions is required. These chemicals cause extensive degradation of cell wall polymers. Wood tanks are, however, satisfactory for holding hydrogen peroxide solutions and give good service on contact with strong brine. Solution of iron salts cause degradation, particularly of the polysaccharides.

In contact with iron under damp conditions, wood may show severe deterioration within a few years. Species high in acidic extractives seem especially prone to such attack. Because traces of iron reduce the brilliance of many dyes, wood tanks have long been preferred to steel in the manufacture of dyes. Similarly, vinegar and sour foodstuffs are processed in wood tanks because common metals impart a metallic taste. Ease of fabrication may be the reason for using wood tanks in less accessible areas to which ready-made tanks of other materials cannot be easily moved.

Resistance to chemical attack is generally improved by resin impregnation, which protects the underlying wood and reduces movement of liquid into the wood. Resistance to acids can be obtained by impregnating with phenolic resin and to alkalies by impregnating with furfural resin.

Bio-deterioration

The principal organisms that degrade wood are fungi, bacteria, insects, and marine borers. Decay, molds, and stain are caused by fungi. Decay is the most serious kind of damage because it causes structural failure and consequently, tremendous economic losses. Soft rot is another type of decay that weakens wood, but it typically progresses slowly and is most often associated with very wet wood. Moisture conditions conducive to decay occur when the moisture content of the wood is above fiber saturation (–30%). The optimum temperature range for most decay fungi is about 25-30 °C, although some species grow at temperatures as low as 0 °C and some as high as 45 °C. The optimum pH is in the range of 4.5 to 5.5. Oxygen is essential for growth of all species. Decay can be prevented by keeping wood either too dry (below 20% moisture content) or too wet (lumens filled with water) for fungal development, by using naturally decay-resistant species, or by treating with preservatives. Mold and stain fungi primarily attack the sapwood. Mold fungi growth occurs primarily on the surface of the wood, while stain fungi may cause a stain throughout the affected sapwood. These fungi can be controlled by dipping the lumber in a fungicidal solution immediately after cutting. Bacterial degradation of wood generally is not a serious problem, although in some situations of extreme wetness, bacteria may increase the permeability of wood after many years or reduce the strength of the wood.

Termites are the most destructive insects that attack wood. Their attack can be prevented or lessened by using naturally resistant wood or by treating wood with preservatives. For sub-terranean termites, which generally require contact with the ground to survive, poisoning the soil around the wood structure is the principal means of preventing infestation. A promising new approach to sub-terranean termite control is the use of food bait with an insecticide. The dry wood termite flies directly to the wood, bores into it, and does not require contact with the ground. Physical barriers, such as paint or screens, prevent infestation. Despite great differences between fungi and termites, chemicals that inhibit fungi usually also inhibit termites.

Marine borers inhabit saline or brackish waters where they cause serious destruction to untreated wood. The mollusks include the Teredo and Bankia borers; among the crustaceans, the Limnoria borers are the most widespread and destructive. Preservatives or borer-resistant woods deter marine borers. For practical purposes, the sapwood of all species may be considered to be susceptible to bio-deterioration. The heartwood of some species, however, contains toxic extractives that protect it against biological attack. Among the native species that have decay-resistant or highly decay-resistant heartwood are bald cypress, redwood, cedars, white oak, black locust, and black walnut. Douglas-fir, several of the pines, the larches, and honey locust are of intermediate decay resistance. Species low in decay resistance include the remainder of the pines, the spruces, true firs, ashes, aspens, birches, maples, hickories, red and black oaks, tupelo, and yellow poplar. Native woods considered somewhat resistant to termite attack include close-grained redwood heartwood and resinous heartwood of southern pine. Although several tropical woods show resistance to marine borers, no commercial native woods are sufficiently borer resistant to be used untreated.

The best protection for wood against the attack of decay fungi, insects, or marine borers is obtained by applying preservatives under pressure before installation. Both oil-type preservatives, such as creosote or petroleum solutions of pentachlorophenol, and waterborne preservatives, such as copper chrome arsenate and ammoniacal-copper arsenate, are used when wood is to be in direct contact with the ground or in the marine environments. Where wood is to be used under low to moderate decay hazard conditions (eg, above ground), it can be protected by brushing, spraying, dipping, or steeping. Once decay is established, preservatives brushed onto the wood will not penetrate, and decay cannot be eradicated in this way. However, high vapour pressure fungicides (fumigants) penetrate deeply into wood and have successfully stopped internal decay in structural timbers. Diffusible preservatives such as boron and fluoride are also used to eradicate decay.

(b) Plywood

Plywood is made by bonding together a number of thin sheets or veneers of wood. The grain in adjacent plies is oriented at right angles, and an odd number of plies are used. The main purpose of plywood is to overcome the directional properties of wood, thereby obtaining a material more uniform in all directions. Plywood shows greater resistance to checking and splitting than lumber and has better dimensional stability because of reduced shrinkage and swelling. It is classed as interior or exterior depending on the type of adhesive used to bond the plies together. Interior grade usually is bonded with water soluble glues and thus has limited resistance to moisture. Exterior grade is completely waterproof in that it can withstand prolonged immersion in water without disintegration.

(c) Cellulose Derivatives

Cellulose is a naturally occurring high polymer found in all woody plant tissue and in such materials as cotton. It can be modified by chemical processes into a variety of thermoplastic materials, which in turn may be still further modified with plasticizers, fillers, and other additives to provide a wide variety of properties. The oldest of all plastics is cellulose nitrate.

(i) Cellulose Acetate

It is the basis of safety film, developed to overcome the highly flammable nature of cellulose nitrate. Starting as film, sheet, or molding powder, it is made into a variety of items, such as transparent package and a large variety of general purpose items. Depending on the plasticizer content, it may be hard and rigid or soft and flexible. Moisture absorption of this and all other cellulosics is relatively high and they are therefore not recommended for long continued outdoor exposure. But cellulose acetate film, reinforced with metal mesh, is widely used for temporary enclosures of buildings during construction.

(ii) Cellulose Acetate Butyrate

It is a butyrate polymer, is inherently softer and more flexible than cellulose acetate and requires less plasticizer to achieve a given degree of softness and flexibility. It is made in the form of clear transparent sheets and film or in the form of molding powders which can be molded by standard injection molding procedures into a wide variety of products. Like the other cellulosics, this material is inherently tough and has good impact resistance. It has infinite colourability, like the other cellulosics. Cellulose acetate butyrate tubing is used for such application as irrigation and gas lines.

(iii) Ethyl Cellulose

It is similar to cellulose acetate and acetate butyrate in its general properties. Two varieties, general purpose and high impact are common, high impact ethyl cellulose is made for better than average toughness at normal and low temperatures.

(iv) Cellulose Nitrate

It is one of the toughest plastics, is widely used for tools handles and similar applications requiring high impact strength. Its high flammability requires great caution, particularly when the plastics in the form of film. Most commercial photographic films are made of cellulose nitrates rather than safety film. Cellulose nitrate is the basis of most of the widely used commercial lacquers for furniture and similar items.

(d) Plastics

The synonymous terms plastics and synthetic resins denote synthetic organic high polymers are compounds in which the basic molecular level sub-units are long chain molecules. The word of plastic has been adopted as a general name for the group of materials because all are capable of being molded at some stage in their manufacture. The mechanical behaviour of a plastic is generally affected the internal structure of the polymer. The elastic moduli of plastics generally range from 10^4 to 10^6 psi, considerably lower than for metals. The greater strains observed when plastics are loaded result from the fact that there is chain straightening in polymers as well as bond lengthening. Permanent deformation in plastics occurs as slip between adjacent molecular chains. Plastics are divided into two large categories based on their thermal behaviour: thermoplastic and thermosetting materials.

(i) Thermoplastic Materials

These material extremely plastic, that is, easily deformable, at elevated temperatures. They become hard again on cooling. They can be so softened by heating and hardened by cooling any number of times. Thermoplastic resins deform easily under applied pressures, particularly at elevated temperatures and so are used to make molded products. Materials in this category can be repeatedly softened by heating and hardened by cooling. The main varieties of thermoplastics are as following:

Acrylics

Acrylics in the form of large transparent sheets are used in aircraft enclosures and building constructions. Although not so hard as glass, acrylics have perfect clarity and transparency. They are the most resistant of the plastics to sunlight and outdoor weathering and they have an optimum combination of flexibility and rigidity with resistance to shattering. Sheets of acrylic are readily formed to complex shapes. They are used for such applications as transparent windows, outdoors and indoors signs, parts of lighting equipments, decorative and functional automotive parts, reflectors, household appliances parts and similar applications.

Acryl-Butadienenitril-Sryrene (ABS)

ABS is a three way copolymer that provides a family of tough, hard, chemically resistant resins. The greatest use is for pipes and fittings.

Polycarbonate

It has excellent transparency, high resistance to impact and good resistance to weathering. It is used for safety glazing, general illumination and hard hats.

Polyethelene

In its unmodified form is a flexible, waxy, translucent plastic maintaining flexibility at very low temperatures in contrast with many other thermoplastic materials. It is highly inert to most solvents and corrosive chemicals of all kinds at ordinary temperatures. It is widely used as a primary insulating material on wire and cable and has been used also as replacement for the lead jacket on communication cables and other cables.

Polypropylene

It is a polyolefin, is similar in many ways to its counterpart, polyethylene, but is generally harder, stronger and more temperature resistant. It has a great many uses among them for complete water cisterns for water closets in plumbing systems abroad.

Polytetrafluoroethylene

Polytetrafluoroethylene, with the very active element fluorine in its structure, is a highly crystalline linear type polymer, unique among organic compounds in its chemical inertness and resistance to change at high and low temperatures. This material is not embrittled at low temperatures and its films remain flexible at temperatures below 100°F. It is used in bridges as beam seats or bearings and in buildings calling for resistance to extreme conditions, or for applications requiring low friction. In steam lines, for example, supporting pads of Polytetrafluo-roethylene permit the line to slide easily over the pads as expansion and contraction with changes in temperature cause the line to lengthen and shorten. The temperatures involved have little or no effect.

Polyvinyl Fluoride

It has much of the superior inertness to chemical and weathering attack typical of the fluorocarbons. Among other uses, it is used as thin-film overlays for building boards to be exposed outdoors.

Polyvinyl Formal Resins

Polyvinyl resins are used principally as a base for tough, water-resistant insulating enamel for electric wire.

Polyvinyl Butyral

It is the tough interlayer in safety glass. In its cross-linked and plasticized form, polyvinyl butyral is used extensively in coating fabrics for raincoats, upholstery and other heavy duty moisture-resistant applications.

Vinyl Chloride Polymers and Copolymers

They vary from hard and rigid to highly flexible. Polyvinyl chloride is naturally hard and rigid but can be plasticized to any required degree of flexibility, as in raincoats and shower curtains. Copolymers including vinyl chloride plus vinyl acetate are naturally flexible without plasticizers. Non-rigid vinyl plastics are widely used as insulation and jacketing for electric wire and cable because of their electrical properties and resistance to oil and water. Heavy gauge sheets are widely used as upholstery. Vinyl chlorides are used for floor coverings in the form of tile and sheet because of their abrasion resistance and relatively low water absorption. The rigid materials are used for tubing, pipe and other applications which require resistance to corrosion and action of many chemicals, especially acids and alkalis; they are attacked by a variety of organic solvents.

Vinylidene Chloride

It is highly resistant to most inorganic chemicals and organic solvents generally. It is impervious to water on prolonged immersion and its films are highly resistant to moisture-vapour transmission. It can be sterilized. It is not recommended for uses involving high speed impact, shock resistance or flexibility at sub-freezing temperatures. It should not be used in applications requiring continuous exposure to temperatures in excess of 170°F.

Polystyrene Formulations

They constitute a large and important segment of the entire field of thermoplastic materials. It is one of the lightest of the presently available commercial plastics. It is relatively inexpensive and easily molded and has good dimensional stability and good stability at low temperatures. It is brilliantly clear when transparent but can be produced in an infinite range of colours. Water absorption is negligible even after long immersion. Electrical characteristics are excellent. It is resistant to most corrosive chemicals, such as acids and a variety of organic solvents although it is attacked by others.

Under certain circumstances they tend to develop fine cracks, known as craze marks in highly stressed conditions.

Polyimide

Polyimide, in molded form, is used in increasing quantities for impact and high resistance to abrasion. It is employed in small gears, cams, and other machine parts because even when unlubricated, polyimide is highly resistant to wear. Its chemical resistance, except to phenols and mineral acids, is excellent. Extruded polyimide is coated on to electric wire, cable and rope for abrasion resistance.

(ii) Thermosetting Materials

These materials are either originally soft at once upon heating but upon further heating they harden perma-nently. The final, continuous framework structure of thermosetting resins may develop from the condensation polymerization mechanism or may harden by the formation of the primary bonds between molecular chains as thermal energy is applied. In general thermosetting plastics are stronger than thermoplastic resins, particularly at elevated temperatures. Amorphous polymers have a characteristic temperature at which the properties make a drastic change, called the glass transition temperature. The transition from glassy behaviour to rubbery behaviour may occur at any temperature.

Phenol Formaldehyde

It provides the greatest variety of thermosetting molded plastic articles. They are used for chemical decorative, electrical, mechanical and thermal appliances of all kinds. Hard and rigid, they change slightly, if at all, on aging indoors but on outdoor exposure lose their bright surface gloss. However, the outdoor exposure characteristics of the more durable formulations are otherwise generally good. Phenol formaldehyde has good electrical properties, do not burn readily, and do not support combustion. They are strong, light weight and generally pleasant to the eye and touch. Light colours normally are not obtainable because of the dark brown basic colour of the resin. They have low water absorption and good resistance to attack by most commonly found chemicals.

Furan Resins

Furan resins are similar to phenolics in many respects. Touch and durable, they have many industrial uses, such as for large aggregate filled molds for shaping light metals.

Cast Phenolics

Cast phenolics were once used in large quantities for brilliantly coloured parts, but today they are used principally in industrial applications, including molds.

Epoxy and Polyester Resins

They are used for a variety of purposes. For example, electronic parts with delicate components are sometimes cast completely in these materials to give them complete and continuous support and resistance to thermal and mechanical shock. Some varieties must be cured at elevated temperatures; others can be formulated to be cure at room temperatures. One of the outstanding attributes of the epoxies is their excellent adhesion to a variety of materials, including such metals as copper, brass, steel and aluminium.

Polyester Molding Materials

When compounded with fibers (particularly glass fibers) or with various mineral fibers (including clay), can be formulated into putties or premixes that is easily compression or transfer molded into parts having high impact resistance.

Melamine Formaldehyde Materials

They are unaffected by common organic solvents, grease and oils and most weak acids and alkalis. Their water absorption is low. They are insensitive to heat and are highly flame resistant, depending on the filler. Electrical properties are particularly good, especially resistance to arcing. Unfilled materials are highly translucent and have unlimited colour possibilities. Principle fillers are alpha cellulose for general purpose compounding; minerals to improve electrical properties, particularly at elevated temperatures; chopped fabric to afford high shock resistance and flexural strength; and cellulose, used mainly for electrical purposes.

Polyurethane

It is used several ways in construction. As thermal insulation, it is used in the form of foam; either pre-foamed or foamed in place. The latter is particularly useful in irregular spaces. When blown with fluorocarbons, the foam has an exceptionally low Lambda factor and is therefore widely used in thin walled refrigerators. Others uses include field applied or baked on clear or coloured coatings and finishes for floors, walls, furniture and casework generally. The rubbery form is employed for sprayed or trowelled on roofing and for gaskets and calking compounds.

Alkyds

Alkyds are customarily combined with mineral or glass fillers, the latter for high impact strength. Extreme rapidly and completeness of cure permit rapid production of large number of parts from relatively few molds. Because electrical properties, especially resistance to arcing, are good, many of the applications for alkyd molding materials are in electrical applications.

Urea Formaldehydes

Urea formaldehydes, like the melamines, offer unlimited translucent to opaque colour possibilities, light fastness, good mechanical and electrical properties and resistance to organic solvents and mild acids and alkalis. Although there is no swelling or change in appearance, the water absorption of urea formaldehyde is relatively high and therefore it is not recommended for applications involving long exposure to water. Occasional exposure to water has no deleterious effect. Strength properties are good.

Silicones

Silicones, unlike other plastics, are based on silicon rather than carbon. As a consequence, their inertness and durability under a wide variety of conditions are outstanding. As compared with the phenolics, their mechanical properties are poor and consequently glass fibers are added. Molding is more difficult than with other thermosetting materials. Unlike most other resins they may be used in continuous operations at 400°F; they have very low water absorption; their dielectric properties are excellent over an extremely wide variety of chemical attack; and under outdoor conditions their durability is particularly outstanding. In liquid solutions, silicones are used to impart moisture resistance to masonry walls and to fabrics. They also form the basis for a variety of paints and other coatings capable of maintaining flexibility and inertness to attack at high temperatures in the presence of ultra violet sunlight and ozone. Silicone rubbers maintain their flexibility at much lower temperatures than other rubbers.

Plasticizers and Fillers

Plasticizers and fillers may be added to polymers to change their basic properties. Plasticizers are low-molecular-weight (short-chain) substances added to reduce the average molecular weight of a polymer and thus make it more flexible. Fillers may be added, particularly to the softer plastics to stiffen them, increase their strength and impact properties, or improve their resistance to heat. Wood flour, mica, asbestos, fibers and chopped fibers or fabric may be used as filler material for polymers.

(e) Asphalt

Asphalt materials have been known and used in road and building construction since ancient times. Early asphalt was of natural origin, found in pools and asphalt lakes, but current supplies come mainly from the residues of refined petroleum. It is black or dark brown petroleum derivative, is distinct from tar, the residue from destructive distillation of coal. Asphalt consists of hydrocarbons and their derivatives and is completely soluble in carbon disulfide. Asphalt and asphalt products are also used extensively in roofing applications. Asphalt is used as a binder between layers in built up roofing and as the impregnating agent in roofing felts, roll roofing and shingles. Care should be taken not to mix asphalt and tar together, that is, to place asphalt layers on a tar insulated felt or vice-versa, unless their compatibility has been checked.

(i) Bituminous Pavements

Asphalt refined to meet specifications for paving purposes is called asphalt cement. At normal temperatures it is semisolid. Several types of asphalts are produced as; Rapid Curing (RC) asphalt, medium curing asphalt and slow curing asphalt and emulsified asphalt.

(ii) Asphalt Building Products

It is water resistant and durable therefore, used for many building applications. For damp proofing and water proofing, three types of asphalt are used: Type A, an easy flowing, soft, adhesive material for use underground or in other moderate temperature applications. Type B, a less susceptible asphalt for use above ground where temperatures do not exceed 125°F and Type C, for use above ground where exposed on vertical surface to direct sunlight or in other areas where temperatures exceed 125°F.

It is evident from the above literature that there is a wide variety of organic building materials available. They together make a place to be lived in. Their use in construction is right from civilization of man, but the forms and use of the materials is changing as per the advances in the life.

2.2 Environmental Factors Affecting Indoor Housing Conditions

On the basis of studies of Ashton in 1969; Anonymous (1999); Miral *et al.* (2003); Kenjo (2005) and Vadstrup (2005) an interesting fact about the organic building materials was delineated that the durability of materials used in building and subsequently exposed to weather is of great interest to the architects, the builders and the ultimate users. A brief description of the effects of weather on organic building materials classed is given below:

(a) Weathering

The process of weathering is defined as the action of atmospheric elements in altering the colour, texture, composition or form of exposed objects, ultimately leading to disintegration or failure to perform a function.

Radiation from the sun at the earth's surface is composed of near ultraviolet, visible and near infrared portions of the spectrum. Moisture results from rain (or snow), water vapour (humidity), and condensed water vapour (dew or frost). Thermal aspects of the weather relate to the presence or absence of heat (high or low temperatures) and the rapidity of change from one condition to the other (thermal shock).

Gases that can enter into the weathering process directly are the normally present oxygen and carbondioxide, plus pollutants such as ozone, sulphur dioxide and oxides of nitrogen.

(i) Radiation

Organic building materials are chiefly composed of long-chained molecules with carbon-to-carbon backbones. These are attracted to each other by secondary forces, although if the material is "cross-linked" there are also chemical bonds between the long chains. The amount of energy required to break these primary bonds and thus disrupt the individual molecules can be calculated. As the wavelength of radiation decreases, its energy increases and reaches the breaking energy of the carbon bonds at a wavelength of 350 nm. This is well within the range of solar radiation received at sea level. Fortunately, the proportion of shorter wavelength radiation is small at the earth's surface so that the intensity of the most destructive wavelengths is very much reduced. Ultraviolet makes up about 10 per cent of the sun's radiant energy, but at the earth's surface at noon it provides 5 to 7 per cent of the energy; biologically active UV is about one per cent of the total energy. These proportions decrease markedly before and after noon because of atmospheric scattering at lower angles. If this were not the case, no organic material would have any exterior durability.

The degradation of organic building materials attributable to UV can take two paths. With some, the energy starts a process the reverse of the polymerization reaction that produced the large molecules. This is the so-called "unzipping" of the polymer that leads to catastrophic failure. As it is a chain reaction, the aim of materials chemists is to prevent it from starting, a task much easier to state than to accomplish. The inclusion of pigments that reflect the UV or absorb it preferentially to the polymer is the most common remedy; e.g., carbon black in polyethylene. In the other degradation mechanism, the smaller molecules produced by chain scission frequently react across the chains. This results in more cross-linking than was originally present so that the material becomes harder and more brittle. If some flexibility is required for the material to perform its function, the induced brittleness causes cracking. Most organic building materials fail in this manner. On a gross scale, it is called cracking; on a reduced scale, with a rectangular pattern, it is called checking. On plastics, on a small scale, the result is referred to as crazing, while with coatings microscopic cracking leads to chalking as the top layer erodes away.

Even though the organic material itself may be resistant, it is possible for UV light to cause undesirable changes if the material is coloured and the colorant, many of which are organic, is not resistant. Fading, which is usually not acceptable, will occur. UV can also cause yellowing. It may alter a resin's chemical structure so that it absorbs blue visible light and appears to be yellow. Fortunately in many cases visible light has the effect of bleaching these induced colours.

As only short wavelength radiation possesses sufficient energy to break the primary bonds, it follows that longer wavelengths can only directly affect the secondary forces. Visible and infrared radiation leads chiefly to increased temperature and thus to softening in materials that do not contain much cross-linking. The indirect effect is to increase the rate of chemical reactions that may be occurring from other causes. This increase in temperature due to solar radiation can be substantial.

(ii) Moisture

Water is one of the most prevalent elements of weather. Because most organic building materials are hydrophobic and not porous, they are not so readily damaged by the freezing action of water as are many inorganic materials.

Wood, being composed of a hydrophilic polymer in cellular form is readily swollen by water. The polymer however, does not dissolve in or react with water, so that wood docs not disintegrate when swollen, even if later frozen. Water is necessary for the degradation of wood by micro-organisms, even though one type is called "dry" rot.

Some organic coatings intended for use on wood, particularly oil paints pigmented with zinc and titanium oxides, swell markedly when immersed in water. When water (from either the exterior or the interior of a building) collects at the back of such a paint film, it expands in area more than the corresponding substrate and is forced off the surface, with resultant blisters. Water can also cause blistering

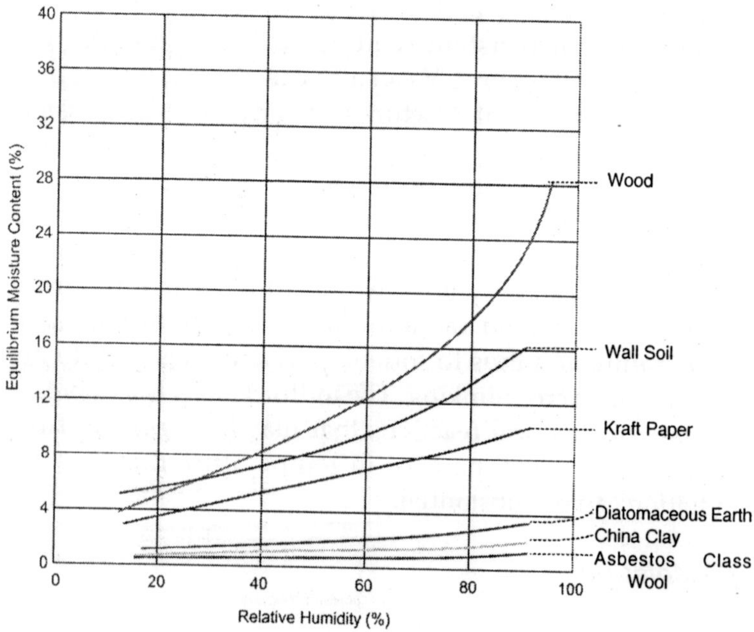

Figure 2.1: Moisture Content of some Construction Materials (Kenjo, 2005)

of coatings that swell only slightly if more moisture collects at the interface than can be transmitted through the film. When the hydrostatic pressure exceeds the adhesive strength of the film, blistering occurs. Swelling properties, permeability and adhesion to moist surfaces have, therefore, been considered important parameters in the assessment of exterior coatings for wood. Moisture can cause degradation of coatings on metal if it can permeate the film and initiate corrosion, the products of which can disrupt the coating.

Roofing materials, which are used for their waterproofing ability, and plastics are generally little affected by water. Glass-reinforced plastics can be damaged if the fibres are too close to the surface or the resin weathers away, allowing water to wick along the fibres and reduce the reinforcing action. Frozen water in the form of hail can damage brittle plastics by impact. Sealants in the bulk are unaffected by water, but their adhesion can be destroyed if water attains access to the interface. Such failures occur most often on porous substrates that can absorb water.

(iii) Temperature

Temperature can have both a physical and a chemical effect. Physically, a change in temperature alters such attributes as hardness and strength, which are related to the tensile properties of the material. A temperature increase softens materials that do not contain much cross-linking between the molecules, i.e., the thermoplastics. Those that are highly cross-linked usually decompose before much softening occurs; these are the thermoset materials.

Decrease in temperature increases the hardness or modulus of organic building materials and if they become too hard they may not perform their function properly. In addition, a sudden change in temperature in either direction can cause internal stresses in thick sections owing to the low rate of heat transmission of most organic materials. With such a change, the outer surface responds quickly to the new conditions while the inner portion is still at the original temperature. Thermal shock can thus lead to surface cracking if the exterior contracts rapidly while the interior is expanded, or to interior cracking under the reverse conditions. Chemically, temperature changes the rate of reactions. Oxidation, which is a slow reaction at room temperature with most materials, takes place much more quickly at elevated temperatures.

After coatings have been cured, low temperatures do not affect them particularly unless they are subjected to impact. Neither does higher temperatures experienced in weathering have any direct effect. Because coatings are applied in thin films, thermal shock is not generally important.

Sealants that have been properly formulated resist the forces exerted by high temperatures (softening of the material and thermal expansion of the jointed units), which tend to make them flow. Low temperatures, such as those experienced in many parts of Canada, place extreme demands upon sealants because they must elongate most when they are least able, owing to hardening or stiffening. Rate of temperature change is also important because organic materials, in general, can accommodate slow rates of strain much more readily than fast rates of strain.

Plastics designed for use in buildings are not softened in hot weather, although the ability of thermoplastics to support a load may be reduced owing to creep. Low temperatures make them stiffer but most do not become brittle. Rigid (unplasticized) polyvinyl chloride, which is only used where extreme chemical resistance is required, and polymethyl methacrylate, which has good clarity, already has little impact resistance because they are in the glassy state at normal temperature. Thermal shock, especially when cyclical, can cause cracking or exudation of plasticizer from plastics.

Temperature extremes also place demands upon asphaltic and tar roofing materials. If a hard material is used so that it will not flow in the summer sun, it may become brittle and crack badly at low temperatures, and *vice-versa*. Thus the selection of the proper grade requires considerable care. Because of the need to resist flow at high temperatures, the material can only withstand low temperature shrinkage that is uniformly distributed, emphasizing the importance of design. Moderate flow at high roof temperatures is designed to overcome small cracks caused by low temperatures.

(iv) Gases

The atmospheric gas most damaging to organic materials because of its high concentration and reactivity is oxygen. Chemical linkages that are not completely "saturated" or satisfied (chemically called double bonds) are particularly susceptible to oxidation. Indeed, this is the basis of the drying mechanism of oil paints and other coatings that cure through oxidative polymerization. Because it is impossible to have a binder that contains the exact number of double bonds to cause solidification but no more, the reaction continues past the optimum stage and becomes part of the degradation process. Hence, oil paints, which depend solely upon this drying process, are more susceptible to continued oxidation than coatings, which include other methods of polymerization, e.g., alkyds.

Natural and many synthetic rubbers contain unsaturation and consequently oxidize, leading to discoloration, hardening, crazing and finally cracking. Unsaturation, however, is not essential for oxidation; polymers that contain reactive hydrogen atoms are also attacked: polystyrene and polyethylene, for example. Because oxygen must diffuse into the material to continue the reaction, oxidation often occurs only at the surface unless the material is in a thin film.

The other major gases, carbondioxide and nitrogen, do not react with organic building materials and are frequently used in chemical synthesis as inert atmospheres. Rapid movement of the normal atmosphere, wind, can cause weathering by impinging rain, sand or dust upon exposed surfaces. Degradation of coatings is usually more severe on the sides of buildings that bear the brunt of storms.

Ozone is normally present only in the upper atmosphere and can be considered a pollutant at ground level. Being an unstable modification of oxygen, containing three instead of the normal two atoms, it is extremely reactive. Materials that oxidize will therefore react with ozone. An illustration of this is ozone-cracking of rubbers. Sulphur dioxide, present in industrial atmospheres from the burning of sulphur-containing fuels, is the other common pollutant. Its action is to form sulphuric acid, which may diffuse through organic coatings and attack the underlying metal.

(b) Earthquakes

Earthquakes are, perhaps, the most unpredictable environmental hazard. Perhaps the biggest irony of the moment is that earthquakes do not kill people but buildings do. A survey carried out of the Chamoli earthquake found that the structure with cross ties performed satisfactorily. In the earthquake prone Uttaranchal hills, folk wisdom places great emphasis on quality of construction. Apart from the proper selection of sites, the foundation was laid using the interlocking technique (*Jor-tor*) in which stones were wielded with one flat stone and the space between was filled with fine rock pieces. Similar attention was paid to the corners. No wonder many temples have managed to survive the quakes that shake the area routinely. The survey of the different parts of greater Himalaya indicated that the inhabitants constructed their houses with the designed anti-seismic arrangement. They might be the sufferer of earthquake in the past; hence they applied indigenous technique of house construction. The building weight was distributed into different components with horizontal and vertical wooden beams embedded into the stone-masonry wall. Such type of structures can be seen in the entire hill region of Uttaranchal. Due to this design some of the triple storied traditional buildings successfully survived several seismic shocks in the last century.

(c) Combinations

Two elements of weather, acting together, almost invariably produce greater deterioration than either one alone. There are many examples of this synergistic action. When UV breaks a polymer chain, water can remove low molecular weight materials that could act as plasticizers, thus adding to the brittleness caused by cross-linking. Leaching by water of irradiated lignin is responsible for the graying of exposed wood. Materials that have been irradiated oxidize much faster than those that have not, and photo-oxidation is one of the chief reactions in degradation. Most polymers are much more stable to heat in the absence of oxygen than they are in its presence; and more stable to oxygen in the absence of heat. For example, toughened polystyrene can be heated at 260 °C for 20 hours without change, but in air either heat or UV cause yellowing and embrittlement at lower temperatures. Plastics softened by heat are more readily eroded by wind-driven sand. Both oxygen and water are involved in the rusting of iron, which disrupts organic coatings. Ozone cracking occurs sooner when the material is under mechanical stress. If three elements act together, the result is even more complicated.

Norwegian studies by Mattson and Oftedal in 2005 indicate quite clearly that the decay of wood due to natural exposure is more or less predictable. One explanation is the traditionally use of pine logs with an extensive amount of heartwood, which ensure a clear limitation regarding to growth of wood-decaying fungi and wood-boring insects. Another reason for long service life of wood is the "favourable" climate (a combination of generally low precipitation and low temperature) and constructions based on long-term experience. Inserting protection layers, such as cladding outside the log construction has a traditional development through the 18th and 19th century. At the same time, expanding use of surface treatment by tar products, oil paint, linseed-oil paint and stains gave further protection from humidity and prolonged the service life. "Unpredicted" or extensive decay is often due to relatively clear events/ change in exposure (Figure 2.2).

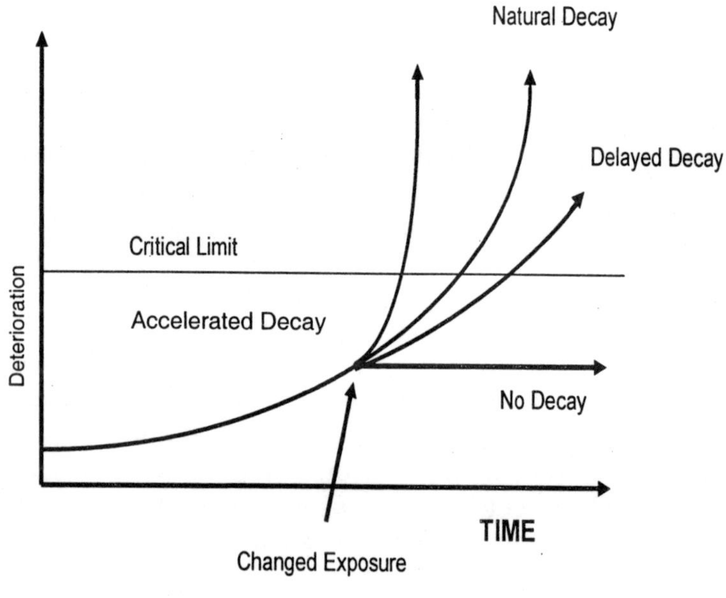

Figure 2.2: Service life, depending on change of exposure (Mattson and Oftedal, 2005)

Therefore, the above factors collated following five causes for most of the deterioration and damages (Plate-2.2) in the organic building materials:

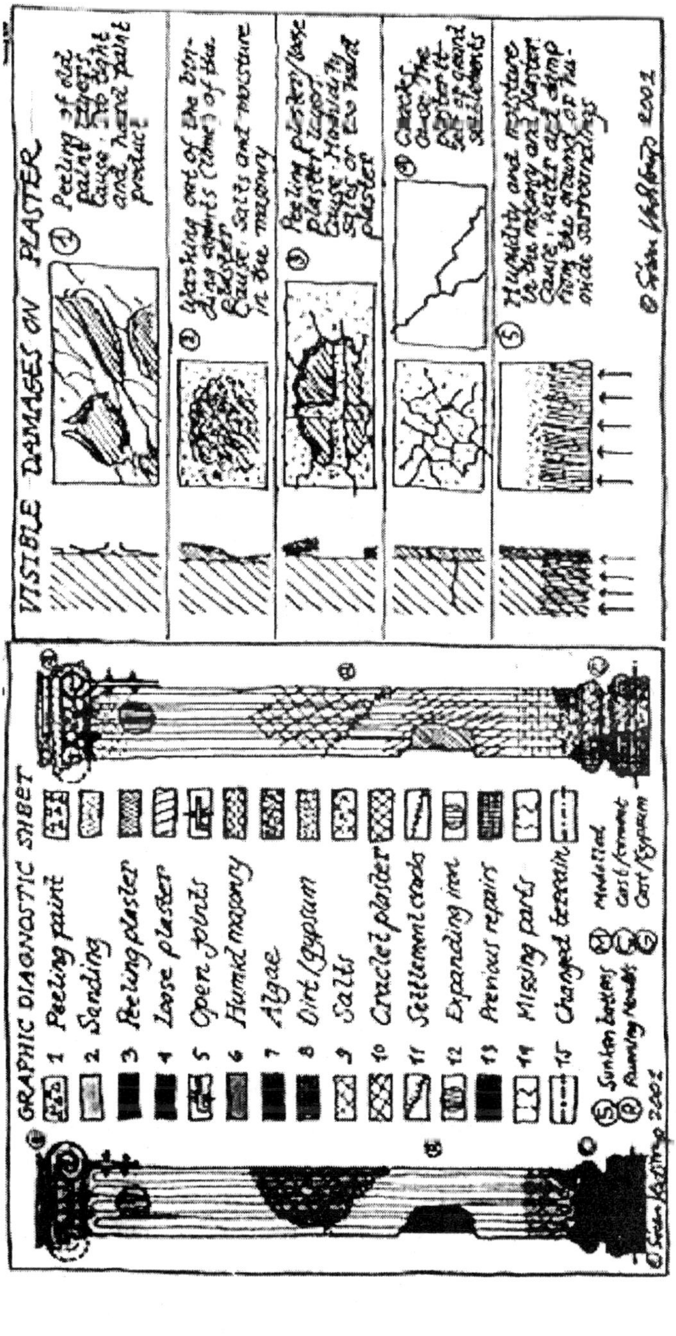

Plate 2.2 : Graphic diagnose sheet of visible deterioration and damages (Vadstrup, 2005)

6. *Influence of Water* : and the consequences or followers of water: Moisture, ice, saltwater, acid rain. This causes dry rot and fungus in wood, salts in masonry and stones, frost damages, acid deterioration, algae, dirt etc.
7. *Mechanical Causes* : from wear, ground decreases, insufficient carrying capacity and wind.
8. *Technical Faults:* from insufficient constructions: Leakages, insufficient adjoints between materials, too hard and moisture tight surface treatments or finishing coats, changes in the physical balance in the constructions.
9. *Forced Deterioration* : of the surface materials due to leakages in the roof, joints, watertight surface on iron etc.
10. *Other Causes* : incorrect use and arrangements, neglect of maintenance.

The literature cited above made it evident that the well-known elements of weather; radiation, moisture, thermal conditions, gases and earthquakes, etc. affect life and performance of building materials further affecting indoor environment. Changed use (no more heating, lack of maintenance) or construction of the buildings (new materials, thermal insulation) may be the factors that provoke an accelerated rate of decay. Even small changes, such as applying a modern paint system, can be sufficient for a major change in rate of decay.

2.3 Review of Studies Conducted in India and Abroad

Organic materials used on or in buildings can be classified according to their use (Ashton, 1969) which further makes a housing environment. Environment living conditions, including housing conditions, are among the primary determinants of an individual's health, thus its performance have attracted the interest of public health scientist since ancient times (Foster, 1992; Ineichen, 1993 and Krieger, 2002). Some of the studies for the interest of the present research have been summarized as under:

(a) Review of Studies on Organic Building Materials

Gudkin et al. (1971) have felt that four main classes of natural polymeric compounds are poly saccharides, proteins, fats and lipids and the information encoded polydeoxyribose nucleic acid and polyribonucleic acid (DNA and RNA). The properties of these compounds are important for understanding cellular functions and for the utilization of the cells for bio-conversions.

It was found by *Kirk (1975)* that polystyrene can be changed to bio-degradable monomers introducing some functional groups which are characteristic of lignin into benzene ring.

Review of *Carlisle (1976)* includes utilization for electric power generation, home heating and insulation, chemical extractives etc. the 'Energy Forest' concept is analyzed; it involves the management of an entire forest area for continuous harvesting and subsequent conversion to energy. It is concluded that utilization for fuelling large power plants is not economically attractive at present, but that there is potential for small scale power production and for the use of mill residues to provide mill energy. The conversion of forest biomass to liquid and gaseous fuels is technically possible but costs are high. The potential is discussed for the utilization of forest products for medicinal and chemical extractives and for fodder. It is suggested that energy could be conserved by the use of wood in house construction instead of metals and plastics needing large amounts of energy to manufacture. Methods to increase yields for such uses are discussed and their social and environmental implications are considered.

Dinwoodie (1977), in his study found out that the loss in

strength and stiffness occurred in unstressed UF chipboard cycled between 30 per cent and 90 per cent RH at 25 °C may be due to chemical or mechanical degradation of the adhesive. The results of strength tests on thin, cast films of UF adhesives, having a range of formaldehyde to urea ratios, exposed to cyclic humidity changes at 20 °C, indicate that the loss in strength and stiffness is unlikely to be due to chemical changes in the adhesive. Similar results were obtained with adhesive films stored in the presence of sawdust. The method of preparing thin, clear, cast films of uniform thickness is described.

Stryer (1981) studied that wood has been in use as a construction material while several gadgets made from natural organic materials like leather gaskets, felt packing, fibre bending and oil lubricants are being used. Efforts are continuously being made to improve the engineering properties of organic materials. Development of plywood has overcome the non-uniformity in wood and still better physical properties are obtained when the pores of wood are impregnated with a thermosetting resin. The ingenuity of technologies in working with organic materials improved the engineering properties of natural as well as synthetic polymers. Great strides have been made and continue to be made in the utilization of such materials.

Razek et al. (1984) presented in his paper about a thermal investigation of traditional house tested experimentally under the effect of external climatic conditions of hot dry region in Egypt (Toshky region). The external and internal walls of the test house were constructed from local sandstones blocks with 50 cm thick. The ratio between the external openings and the external walls surfaces areas is less than 20 per cent. The external wall is covered internally with 2-3 cm cement mortar plaster, while the internal walls covered with 2-3 cm cement plaster from both sides. Volts and domes covered the roof of the test house. The external surface of the roof covered with 2-3 cm white cement mortar plaster. The results of the investigation demonstrated that, the local building materials such as sandstone suppress the swing of external outdoor air temperature and stabilize the indoor air temperature at average level below the average of outdoor air temperature by about 2-3 °C only during the hottest period. The results also show that modern insulating materials, together with the local building materials make it possible to maintain the indoor air temperature significantly below the average of the outdoor air temperature by about 4-5 °C and passive cooling systems makes it possible to maintain the indoor air temperature to the thermal human comfort zone or near it. The results showed that evaporate cooling is essentially during the hottest critical period in Toshky region as a passive system.

Webb (1985) presented a discussion on how appropriate building technology can have a significant impact on the transmission of vector borne disease is presented. The earth used in traditional rural housing can be stabilized against erosion, shrinkage and cracking by the addition of bitumen, cement or lime. Stabilized earth can be further improved by compaction in a mechanical press, such as the CINVA ram or the BREPAK machine, or by ramming it firmly with wooden mallets between heavy formers. The use of compressed soil blocks could result in the creation of fewer niches for vector and nuisance arthropods in the domestic environment, as well as better retention of insecticides on their relatively non-porous surfaces.

Bailey et al. (1986) investigated that bio-polymers are polymers produced by living organisms and are either repetitive or non-repetitive in structure. Repetitive bio-polymers like starch and cellulose contain one kind of monomeric unit. Non-repetitive polymers like proteins may contain from several up to 20 different monomer species.

According to *Merritt (1986)* organic materials are perhaps the oldest construction materials. Through many generations of use, people have found ways of getting around some of the limitations of naturally occurring organic construction materials. Plywood for instance has overcome the problem of the highly directional properties of wood. In addition to improving natural materials technologies have developed many synthetic polymers (plastics), which are important in current construction.

Naas (1986) examined the effect of climatic conditions on deterioration of agricultural construction materials for a variety of climates. Concrete was susceptible to excessive deflection of structural members, cracking and corrosion of reinforcement particularly at high temperatures and high relative humidity. Concrete-masonry structures in tropical countries also suffered from thermal stress. Relative corrodibility of steel was compared for 20 dry, tropical, inland, marine, rural and industrial locations throughout the world, with high relative humidity in tropical climates causing corrosion in junctions and welding bands. Wood was particularly susceptible to fungus attack.

A standard procedure was devised by *Zigel* and *Obsedshevskii (1988)* for evaluating the changes in the glossiness, colour, dirtiness, chalking, local bulging, cracking, delamination and break-up of lacquer coverings of fibre boards. All these features are combined by formulae into a single evaluation expressing the resistance of the decorative and protective properties. Data are presented showing the change in the resistance of 5 different lacquer coverings on fibre boards exposed to the air on the roof of a building from 1985 to 1987. The best coverings are identified, and the durations of satisfactory performance are determined.

On the basis of studies in Switzerland, the ecological aspects of the use of timber preservatives were discussed by *Graf (1989)* with regard to the risk of attack by the house longhorn (Hylotrupes bajulus) and the possible dangers from the preservatives. A decision-making diagram is constructed for preservative measures against H. bajulus, aqueous products and organic products.

Lapko et al. (1989) examined degradative processes occurring in wooden ceilings and roofs of a 300 year old building and the changes in strength of the wood resulting from cracking, dry rot and other micro-organisms, wood worm, etc. discussed.

An analysis was made by *Davenne et al. (1996)*, of the failure of joints with dowel type fasteners in glued laminated timber under static loading. The single bolt loaded the wood parallel to the grain. The joint failure was due to cracking along the grain direction. An experimental programme was carried out to investigate joints with different structural parameters and with different bolt diameters. Fracture was analyzed by linear elastic fracture mechanics concepts. Possible pure or mixed modes of fracture were investigated. The crack propagation was assumed to be based on a comparison of the energy release rate with a critical value. An analysis of elastic stresses was carried out for the prediction of the onset of cracking. The critical energy release rate value was obtained from experimental results of fracture tests under three point bending. The comparison between experimental and numerical results for the simulation of fracture in joints showed that the linear elastic fracture mechanics provides a good approximation of load bearing capacity of bolted joints and may help improve design codes.

Challa (1993) has expressed that during the last few decades, polymeric materials have been the fastest growing chemical industry. In the construction industry, we find numerous applications of polymers in piping, resilient flooring, electrical insulation, paints and decorative laminates. The use of polymers now outstrips that of metals on a mass basis.

Ak et al. (1994) studied decontamination of plastic and wooden cutting boards with a view to preventing cross contamination of foods in home kitchens. New and used plastic (four polymers plus hard rubber) and wood (nine hardwoods) boards were cut into 5 cm square blocks (25 sq. cm. area) for these experiments. Bacterial contaminants–Escherichia coli (two non-pathogenic strs plus serotype 0157:H7), Listeria innocua, L. monocy-togenes, or Salmonella typhimurium-applied to the block surface in nutrient broth or chicken juice, were recovered by soaking the surface in nutrient broth or pressing the block onto nutrient agar, within minutes or 12 hours later. Persistence and overnight multiplication of bacteria on plastic surfaces depended on maintenance of humidity so as to prevent drying of the contaminant. New plastic cutting surfaces were relatively easy to clean and were microbiologically neutral, but plastic boards with extensive knife scars were difficult to clean manually, especially if they had deposits of chicken fat on them. Fewer bacteria were generally recovered from wooden blocks than from plastic blocks. Clean wood blocks rapidly absorbed all of the inoculum, after which the bacteria could not be recovered within 3 to 10 min. If the board surface was coated with chicken fat, some bacteria might be recovered even after 12 hours at room temperature and high humidity. Cleaning with hot water and detergent generally removed these bacteria, regardless of bacterial species, wood species, and whether the wood was new or used.

In another research paper, *Ak et al. (1994)*, reported the microbiology of plastic and wooden cutting boards, investigating cross contamination of foods in home kitchens. New and used plastic (four polymers plus hard rubber) and wood (nine hardwoods) cutting boards were cut into 5 cm squares ("blocks"). Escherichia coli (two non-pathogenic strs plus type 0157 : H7), Listeria innocua, L. monocytogenes, or Salmonella typhimurium were applied to the 25 cm^2 block surface in nutrient broth or chicken juice and recovered by soaking the surface in nutrient broth or pressing the block onto nutrient agar, within 3-10 min or upto 12 hours later. Bacteria inoculated onto plastic blocks were readily recovered for minutes to hours and multiplied if held overnight. Recoveries from wooden blocks were generally less than those from plastic blocks, regardless of new or used status; difference increased with holding time. Clean wood blocks usually absorbed the inoculum completely within 3-10 min. If these fluids contained 103-104 c.f.u. of bacteria likely to come from raw meat or poultry, the bacteria might be recovered from wood after 12 hours at room temperature and high humidity, but numbers were reduced by at least 98 per cent and often more than 99.9 per cent. Mineral oil treatment of the wood surface had little effect on the microbiological findings. These results do not support the assertion that plastic cutting boards are more sanitary than wood.

Foster et al. (1994) listed that petrochemical industries produce many types of high polymers among which polyethylene, polypropylene, polystyrene and PVC are most widely made and used. These and other synthetic polymers are very useful as packaging and construction materials because of their physical and chemical properties. However, the disposal of these polymers has become a serious public health problem because they are not easily degraded in nature. Bio-degradation of water soluble polymers is thought to be easier than that of insoluble ones. Polyethylene glycol and PV alcohol for example, are known to be attacked easily by micro-organisms. Oligomers of water insoluble polymers such as polyethylene, polyurethane, aliphatic polyester and nylon-6 are also known to be degraded only with difficulty by micro-organisms. However, polystyrene, which is an aromatic polymer, is resistant to micro-organisms and other bio-deterogenes.

Motohashi (1996) evaluated twenty three kinds of pigment stain coating specifications through the outdoor exposure test. An old type of oil stain made of boiled oil and stain agents, alkyd paint and acrylic emulsion paint were also exposed for comparison. The data obtained show that durability performance levels among the commercial products were remarkably and widely scattered, which is considered to be partly due to lack of material standards. There are many brands of pigment stains on the Japanese market nowadays; however, no material standard is available for distinguishing commercial stains. As to the old type of oil stain, it showed the fastest deterioration among all the specimens. As a result, it can be said that the durability levels of the commercial pigment stains are distinguishable from that of the old type of oil stain although they vary widely. The alkyd paint and the emulsion paint showed little apparent deterioration except for slight chalking within 16 months. On the other hand, some of the pigment stains showed visible deterioration patterns; that is, those specimens showed gradual and fine cracking, peeling and flaking. Such a deterioration pattern is generally considered to be more favourable for repainting than alkyd paints and acrylic emulsion paints which form thicker coated layers and deteriorate unequally.

Oliveira (1997) reported field test results of new tools for triatomine control developed under the sponsorship of WHO/TDR: (1) a slow release formulation of insecticidal paint, containing malathion, applied by spraying; (2) fumigant cans which, when lit, release smokes containing cypermethrin and DDVP (dichlorvos); and (3) sensor boxes for the detection of triatomine infestations. Field assays were performed in Chile, Honduras and Paraguay against Triatoma infestans, T. dimidiate and Rhodnius proxlixus, according to a standard protocol designed by a WHO expert committee. Preliminary 6 months post treatment results for the 3 countries showed efficient vector control when insecticidal paints were used indoors and in the peridomestic environment, keeping reinfestation near to zero. The final results presented for Chile at 2 years post-treatment confirmed the superiority of the slow release insecticidal paints. Sensor boxes were less effective than man hour captures for the detection of infected houses.

Turkulin et al. (1997) analysed weathering of wood and concluded that wood in exterior structures undergoes certain chemical and physical changes which cause the slow degradation of wood surface (weathering). The disintegration is caused by the combined action of ultra violet light from the sun, moisture and oxygen from the air and additional effects of wind, rain and other precipitation. Wood changes colour, roughens and erodes with time. Possible biological attack excluded, weathering is the most serious risk to wood for building purposes. Encouraging the use of wood as the main material for the joinery and other building components depends mainly on the exploitation of the results of research on the improvement of the wood durability, its modifications and its correct and efficient finishing in order to reduce the maintenance costs and extend the service life of protective and decorative coatings.

Cecere et al. (1998) reported the environmental and demographic risk factors associated with the domestic infestation and density of T. infestans in 3 heavily infested rural villagers in Santiago del Estero Province, Argentina, in 1992-94. In a one factor unadjusted analysis, the number of T. infestans captured per person hour was associated significantly and negatively with the use of domestic insecticides by householders, type of thatch used in the roofs and the age of the house and positively with the following: degree of cracking of the indoor walls and presence of hens nesting indoors. In one model, using multiple linear regression and a backward step-wise elimination procedure, most of the variation in the overall abundance of T. infestans was explained by insecticide use and the presence of hens nesting indoors; in another model using the same procedure it was explained by insecticide use, bug density in 1988 and previous spraying with deltamethrin in 1985. Variations in bug density per capture stratum (household goods, beds, walls and roof) were explained by the bug density in other strata and by 1 or 2 of the following risk factors: hens nesting indoors, type of roof, presence of cracks in the walls and number of people living in the house. Bug density might be locally controlled by the availability of refuges in the roofs and walls, by the presence of hens nesting indoors and by the use of domestic insecticides. Certain local materials, such as a grass known as symbol, could be successfully used in rural housing improvement programmes aimed at reducing the availability of refuges for insects in the roof.

According to *Heinrich et al. (1998)* genetic predisposition and indoor exposure to allergens especially during the very early childhood years are major factors for the development of allergic diseases later in life. The present study analysed the association between allergic sensitization in 811 children aged 5-14 years old and residing since birth in homes made of different construction materials. Indoor factors were investigated using a questionnaire and allergic sensitization was assessed by a skin prick test. The prevalence of allergic sensitization was compared between children who lived since birth in 5 different types of building. After adjustment for age, gender, parental education and study area the odds of allergic sensitization were higher among children who lived in prefabricated concrete slab buildings built after 1970 (OR=1.56%, 95% CI=1.02-2.38) and among children who lived in new brick buildings (OR=1.75, 95% CI: 0.88-3.47), than among children who lived in old brick buildings. Moreover, the odds of pollen sensitization was higher among children who lived in the new buildings (prefabricated slab buildings: OR 1.68, 95% CI: 1.04-2.72); new brick buildings: (OR 1.48, 95% CI: 0.64-3.42) while living in timber framed houses associated with higher odds of sensitization against Dermatophagoides farinae and D. pteronyssinus (OR 1.63, 95% CI: 0.77-3.44). The step by step inclusion of single indoor factors like type of heating, numbers of storeys, number of people per room, environmental tobacco smoke, use of gas for cooking purposes, dampness of the home or visible moulds in the logistic regression model only marginally changed the odds ratios. Modern living conditions are associated with higher odds of allergic sensitization.

Johanning et al. (1998) tested samples of building materials (drywall, fibreglass, wallpaper, wood) from various homes or wok places in the USA, which were visibly contaminated with moisture-related fungi, with indirect (feline fetus lung cell assay test) and direct (tetrazolium MTT cleavage test) cytotoxicity screening tests that are particularly sensitive to S. chartarum toxins. In addition, microscopic, chemical, immunochemical (roridin A enzyme immunoassay) and mycological culture analyses were performed. In all cases in which building occupants had reported verifiable skin, mucous membrane, respiratory, central nervous system or neuropsychological abnormalities, cytotoxicity was identified. It is concluded that results of cytotoxicity screening test of field samples, such as the direct MTT test method, will give investigators of health problems related to indoor air quality important toxicity information.

Monroy et. al. (1998) in their study showed the effectiveness of house modification for the control of Chagas' disease vectors under natural and artificial conditions. Wall plastering and paint were evaluated for the control of populations of triatomines by assessing vector numbers in man hour collections before and after modifications in 1993. The authors evaluated 29 houses from 3 small villages in Villa Canales in the Department of Guatemala; 18 of them had some kind of modification or improvement. In houses covered with plastered cement and lime, the authors found a 92 per cent reduction of the total vector population in the following year. Other houses with partial modification and paint with lime showed a reduction of 53 per cent and 35 per cent, respectively. In houses without improvements, the number of vectors remained the same. Triatoma dimidiate and T. nitida were collected in the houses; the infection rates with Trypanosoma cruzi were 21 per cent and 50 per cent, respectively. After the house modifications there were no significant changes in the infection rates. There was no statistical difference in longevity of T. dimidiate when kept under artificial conditions (simulated wall plaster) compared to that observed in the field.

Raghavan, V. (1998) classified building materials in three broad groups according to their nature: Metals and alloys, Ceramics and glasses, Organic polymers. He also stated that organic polymers are relatively inert and light and generally have a high degree of plasticity. Figure 2.3 lists typical examples from each of these three groups of materials.

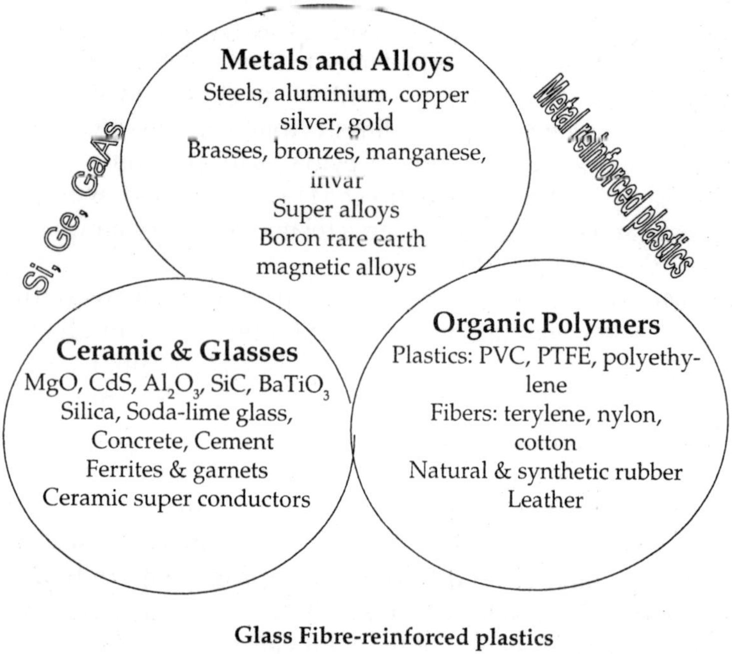

Figure 2.3 : Classification of Engineering Materials (Raghavan, 1998)

Sastry and Radhakrishna (1998) indicated quite clearly that industrial use of rubber includes tyres, tubes protective linings in tanks, pumps, rubber beltings etc. Hand rubber is used in electrical insulating parts, chemically resistant pipes and equipments etc. Foam rubber made by incorporating gas into latex followed by vulcanization is used to make pillows, mattresses, furniture cushions etc. Sponge rubber is produced from rubber by blowing sodium carbonate and injecting fatty acids. Sponge rubber is used sealing, heat insulating, cushioning and shock absorptions. Glues obtained from animal gelatins, vegetables and starches are widely used adhesives. Adhesives made from polymers include cellulose acetate, cellulose acetate butyrates and polysoxylin. These are thermosetting and thermoplastic adhesives Xanthan gum is commercially the most widely produced gum using

Xanthamones compacting. Animal hides contain collogues which can be hydrolyzed into glue or gelatin.

Despot et al. (1999) investigated that the L - joints which were made of home grown Croatian silver fir (Abies alba) sapwood and prepared according to EN 330, were used to establish the influence of coating type and colour on the durability of exterior fir wood joinery. The L-joint's surfaces were treated with two types of coatings and exposed for 36 months in Zagreb. The first type of coat was alkyd paint and the second was stain, both in three different colours; white, brown and black. The L-joints described in this article were not treated with chemical preservatives and were examined after 1, 2, 3, 4, 6, 12 and 36 months of exposure. The influence of coating type was decisive on the moisture contents and permeability during exposure. Regardless of the period of exposure the L-joints coated with stain always had lower average moisture contents and a lower increase in permeability than those coated with the alkyd paint. It happened due to the well known stain vapour diffusively. The influence of the coating type, but it was evident during almost all the exposures. Darker surfaces, particularly during sunny periods absorbed much more heat rays which caused accelerated seasoning, lower moisture content and a smaller increase in permeability.

Trajkovic et al. (1999) in their study reported that chemically untreated pine (Pinus sylvestries) and fir (Abies alba) wood L-joints coated with reference white alkyd paint were exposed outdoors for one year according to EN 330 at two different climatic sites: Garston (UK) and Zagreb (Croatia). Pinewood is the standard reference species for testing the exterior joinery and fir wood is the most frequently used species in the Croatian joinery industry. The aim of the work was to establish the difference between these two species considering the Moisture Content (MC), permeability and bacterial and fungal infection and colonization during exposure. In this article only moisture content, as the main factor of microbial activity and permeability, is presented. The fir wood L-joints mostly had lower MC than the pine L-joints at the same position and site during exposure. In regard to the exposure sites, the differences were larger in Garston than in Zagreb, particularly at the end of exposure. This fact is ascribed to lower natural permeability of fir wood than pinewood, which was emphasized by the specific climatic characteristic of exposure sites. The results indicate that fir sapwood L-joints could also be used in further investigations of home made joinery, wood preservatives and coatings.

The paper by *Yang et al. (2001)* discusses the research conducted on the use of plastic composite in home and abroad and prospect and development trends in wood plastic composite production. Wood plastic composite which is an ideal substitute for wood has more perfect properties than both wood and plastic only. The compounding of wood and plastic separated from solid waste as well as the use of the law of modern composite materials development decreased potential pollution problem in the cities which are caused by waste wood and plastic.

Turkulin and Sell (2002); Wood in exterior conditions undergoes a series of chemical and physical changes that impair its aesthetic appeal and durability. The cladding of the high aesthetic, thermal, other physical and technical demands over a long period of decades, sometimes centuries in use. In order to keep the functional properties of wood unchanged in a long service life, a variety of protective measures may be employed. Physical protection is marked as the most important way to keep the harmful effects of ultra-violet light and precipitation away. Design details of wood products in facades, as well as their assembly means, are considered from the view point of their durability. Chemical protection should generally be avoided, i.e. restricted to a small number of cases when it simply can not be avoided, but surface finishing plays a major aesthetic and technical role in designing and maintaining the wooden facades.

Several efforts by the researchers and engineers have been made to classify engineering materials on the basis of basic structure, origin, use, properties, mechanism, electrical conductivity, etc. It has been investigated that chemical and physical changes impair aesthetic appeal and durability of the building materials and a variety of protective measures could be of great help in keeping them functional. Energy conservation could be practiced by using alternative building materials for naturally occurring building materials.

(b) Housing and Human Performance

Azer, et al. (1972) provides more evidence that hot conditions have significant affects on performance only when they cause a rise in body temperature. In their experiment, performance decrements occurred when subjects worked at 35°C and 75 per cent relative humidity, but not at 35°C or 37.5°C and 50 per cent relative humidity. Relative humidity seems to be a key determinant of performance in a variety of tasks.

Results of research conducted by *Buell etal. (1973)* revealed that skin tests of 546 people in one area revealed 165 (30.2%) reactors but no point source of infection was found after a diagnosed case led to rumours that a focus of infection started the outbreak. In the 2nd community Histoplasma capsulatum was isolated from 10 to 44 soil samples from a wood frequently by starlings. Skin tests conducted on 3750 school children revealed 633 (16.9%) reactors. A higher prevalence of histoplasm in reactors resided near the contaminated woods. Both investigations showed that increased prevalence was associated with males, increased age, farm residence; years lived at residence and play areas in woods, birds' roosts or old buildings.

An infestation of Ornithonyssus bacoti (Hirst) in a farm house in a scattered village near Dresden that was investigated by *Eichler etal. (1973)* is described because they believe it to be typical of many occurring in Eastern Germany.

The farm house was of wood, and the yard was surrounded by buildings. The general appearance was very clean, though rats (Rattus rattus) were present. R. rattus is increasing in numbers in Eastern Germany, occupying niches vacated by R. Norvegicus, which is being intensively controlled. The mites were a serious pest of man every winter, causing severe inflammation of the skin by their bites, particularly in small children who were attacked while asleep. The mites were particularly abundant in the living room. Attempts at control with preparations containing DDT, gamma BHC (lindane) and pyrethrum were unsuccessful.

Christensen (1975) had given a popular account of the harmful effects of fungi in relation to man and animals such as, airborne fungus spores, plant disease and respiratory allergy; fungus predators and parasites of nematodes and insects; fungi pathogenic in man and animals; decay of wood in trees and buildings and fungi.

Annual Report (1977) from Denmark on vertebrate and invertebrate pests of man, domestic animals, building and stored products (including timber) includes sections on advisory work, in which the incidence of enquiries relating to many pests in 1977 as analysed, wood boring pests and their control is on mites, including those in stored grain.

According to *St. Leger and Yarnell (1977) and Smith (1989*) stress and depressive illness are likely to be linked with current housing conditions, as are frequent episodes of acute respiratory illnesses. A long-term implications for health may be experienced many years later, perhaps at a time when current housing conditions are good. There is a growing evidence of an association between frequent or severe bouts of respiratory illness in childhood and lung function in later life.

Allen and Fischer (1978) found that if relative humidity was held constant at 40 per cent, performance on a simple learning task did not vary over range of 11 to 28°C. If relative humidity was not controlled, optimum performance was found to occur at 18 °C, 35 per cent relative humidity. Increase and decrease in temperature lead to performance decrement.

Much of the recent research by *Dunleavy (1981)* has been concerned with public sector housing, especially that which has described as 'mass housing'. It is ironic that local authority housing, a movement which had as one of its most important motivations a desire to improve working class health through better housing conditions has in recent decades produced the new slums and their associated health hazards.

Dias et al. (1982) reported that Government strategy in Brazil for combating Chagas' disease, caused by Trypanosoma cruzi, is directed primarily towards preventing the infestation of houses by the triatomines that are vectors of the pathogen. In practice, this has mainly been restricted to insecticide spraying and transmission in several parts of the States of Sao Paulo and Minas Gerais has been successfully interrupted by this means. However, in the longer term, nearly all infestations could be eliminated in many rural areas by the diligent sealing of the cracks that provide shelter for the triatomines in the adobe walls of house or by the introduction of new building practices that abolish walls prone to cracking. The problems in persuading rural residents to replace the traditional adobe suggested that control of the disease may ultimately depend on the gradual evolution and modification of rural society through the resolution of complex and difficult social problems as well as the provision of new rural housing.

In an another study, the significance of rural housing in the epidemiology and control of Chagas' disease is discussed with reference to studies in two endemic areas, Bambui and Luz, in Minas Gerais State, Brazil. Rural residents tended to resist replacement of their traditional adobe houses, which provide excellent refuges for triatomine bugs and poverty and other factors tended to limit the affected villagers' respectively to both new housing and new methods. However, community participation and other long-term efforts against Chagas' disease in Bambui seem to have increased local awareness of the problem and generated home owners' interest in health related home improvements. Increased awareness among the residents of Esteios, a small community in Luz, appears to have prompted effective local control of Chagas' disease without official government intervention or support.

Pike (1981) and Strachan et al. (1986) defined health and ill health as, if anything, more contentious. In relation to morbidity there is the question of how this is measured–e.g. by demand for medical services, by the detection of clinical symptoms by 'experts' or by asking people themselves? There is some evidence that different methods of measurement produce rather different pictures of the association between poor health and bad housing.

Woodson (1981) has compiled the finding of many studies of the affects of noise on human performance. Although noise level below 90dB (A) is not a serious threat to hearing, they can degrade task performance and cause annoyance.

Pederson and Gravesen (1983), contributed an interesting fact that a woman developed symptoms of headache, swollen and painful joints and breathlessness after moving into a damp house; X-rays indicated nodes in her lungs. The symptoms disappeared spontaneously when she stayed away from the house and secured on her return.

Boardman (1986) and Smith (1989) favoured in case of elderly people, argued that damp, cold houses are an important factor in excess winter deaths in Britain and not just in the extreme form of hypothermia, but also in increased susceptibility to coronary and cerebral thrombosis and respiratory disease.

Byrne et al. (1986) indicated that dramatic improve-ments in housing were accompanied by improvements in health, especially as measured by mortality at younger ages or by the growth and development of children and by a decline in the incidence of those diseases most clearly associated within sanitary and over-crowded housing.

Hunt, Martin and Platt (1986) conducted a research and derived at; women in the damp houses did report significantly more emotional distress. Dampness was, however, strongly related to health problems in children. The mean number of symptoms was higher in children in damp houses, and children in damp houses were more often reported to suffer from aches and pains, diarrhea, nervousness and headaches and to have had atleast one respiratory problem in the past two months. Where there was visible mould growth, there were significantly more reports of vomiting and sore throat in children.

Ineichen (1986) analyzed review on the evidence up to the mid 1980s on the effect of high-rise housing on mental health. It was concluded that 'balance of evidence' suggests a damaging effect, especially for the families with young children

Several studies by *Strachan et al. (1986); McCarthy et al. (1985)* and *Blackman et. al. (1989)* have found links between damp housing, the presence of mould and high rates of asthma and respiratory illness, especially among children.

Blackman et al. (1989) made a comparison in two areas of West Belfast which were both socially and economically deprived, but of which one consisted of very unpopular, high rise, poor-quality dwelling and the other of traditionally built dwellings considered to be significantly better. They found marked differences in mental health between the two areas, for men and children, as well as for women.

Carstairs and Morris (1989) Carstairs in two interesting contributions first proposed the use of : 'an area base for environmental monitoring and epidemiological analysis' and 'the classification of populations by their area of residence appears to offer a superior basis for the explanation of differences in mortality between health boards than does social class'.

The survey of *Glasgow District Council (1989)* indicates quite clearly that dampness has long been a concern of Scots.

In Glasgow, about 70 per cent of homes are known to suffer from dampness/condensation. People living in damp houses tend to believe that this is bad for health and that of their children.

A review of major studies listed by *Smith (1989)* shows, most attention has been paid to respiratory disease (traditionally linked with bad housing), to mental illness, particularly of the depressive type and to general stress induced morbidity. In addition, studies have considered the influence of housing and estate design on the incidence of domestic accidents. Young children, their mothers and elderly people are the groups most often argued to be affected, simply because they spend more time in the home than others.

In *Weekly Epidemiological Record (1990)*, the frequency and geographical distribution of human Trypanosoma cruzi infection in the America is described, dividing the countries with endemic Chagas' disease into 4 groups according to the magnitude of transmission, quantity and quality of the available epidemiological information and existence or non-existence of co-ordinated actions towards the control of this disease. The use of fumigant canisters and insecticidal paints in triatomine control is discussed briefly.

As studied by *Barros (1993)* that ventilation (air speed) is the process of air renewal. The basic purpose of ventilation should be to control the purity of the air. However, with simple ventilation, we control only the speed. For having control on the temperature and the humidity of the air, air conditioner is needed. He also reported that ventilation (air speed) is one of the basic sanitary conditions, because confined air, due to the gases from breathing and transpiration, has its composition altered by lowering the oxygen percentage and increasing that of carbonic gas and the humidity rate. Only with the constant renewal of the air conditions will be made favourable to health, through a normal breathing.

I.I.D.A. (1993) reported that when man is forced to withstand high temperatures, his efficiency drops. Work speed is reduced, the pauses become longer and more frequent, the concentration degree drops and the frequency of error tend to rise significantly, mainly when the temperature reaches 30 °C.

Bredger (1995) stated that good lighting in the home is essential for the comfort and the well-being of all family members. Adequate provision of light is must to avoid wastage in time, energy and strain on the eyes.

Sorensen et al. (1995) concluded that low level of lighting at home contributed to deteriorating mental and physical well-being.

Pires et al. (1999) surveyed 1937 individuals of T. sordida were collected from 196 of 378 domiciliary units sprayed with deltamethrin in July 1995. Intradomicilary infestation occurred in 6 per cent of units and peridomiciliary infestations at 99 per cent of them. 48.3 per cent of the peridomiciliary ecotopes studied were found to be infested, particularly those with wood as the main construction material (constituting 92.1 per cent of the ecotopes in the survey), where 92.5 per cent of the insects were captured, followed by those using adobe (6.2 per cent) , where 3.8 per cent of the insects were captured.

Rudnai et al. (1999) measured the concentrations of formaldehyde, nitrogen dioxide, benzene, xylene and toluene were measured in the homes of school children living in 6 towns in Hungary, whose respiratory health was also assessed by a questionnaire. Passive monitors were used for air sampling. The NO_2 concentration was higher by 75 µg/m^3 in homes with a gas cooker by 80 µg/m^3 in homes with gas heaters and by 27 µg/m^3 in homes with smoking persons than in those without these pollution sources. Busy traffic nearby and gas silicate building material significantly increased the indoor concentration of formaldehyde. The concentrations of benzene and xylene in homes with floor heating or with smoking family members were also higher but due to the limited number of samples, the difference was not statistically significant. The questionnaire data on 1767 3rd grade school children revealed a prevalence of 14.2 per cent of bronchitis type respiratory symptoms. Logistic regression analysis showed significantly higher odds ratios for bronchitis type symptoms with coal/wood cooker (OR=3.64), living density of >2 persons/room (OR=2.05), moulds (OR=2.01), coal/wood oven (OR=1.80), lack of separate children's room (OR=1.62), smoking and a busy traffic nearby (OR=1.33). Asthma type symptoms were associated with moulds in the children's bedroom (OR=2.21), plastic floor covering (OR=1.66) and living density of >2 persons/room (OR=1.49). Allergic symptoms were reported for every 4th child. These were significantly associated with moulds (OR=1.79), shipboard furniture (OR=1.56), concrete building material (OR=1.32) and a busy traffic nearby (OR=1.30). It is concluded that the prevention of the adverse health effects of indoor air pollution should be supported by the enforcement of the hygienic requirements on safe heating and cooking facilities, prevention of indoor mould growing and avoiding of smoking indoors.

As studied by *Bittencourt (2001)*, many different aspects interfere in the environmental climate in the workplace, among them: the impact are on air temperature, radiant temperature, air speed and relative humidity but the type of physical activity is also get affected by clothing that is worn.

Human performance is dynamic and is affected by various personal, demographic as well as environmental factors. Although many efforts have been done to find out effect of housing in terms of temperature, relative humidity, age of building structure, years of occupancy, gender, dampness, etc. it is not very much easy to conclude or draw pictures of the association between poor health and housing. Some of the studies showed the relationship of poor housing conditions and emotional stress, respiratory diseases and other symptoms of poor health. In Indian context, the information provided to draw concrete conclusions is negligible and scanty.

Overview of the literature cited in this chapter delineated following points:

- There is a lot of work has been carried out in India on formulation of new organic building material and their properties, but the knowledge of facts where the critical factors for carry out optimal actions are limited.
- Many of the problems have a universal aspect, even if the single material or climatic situation is unique. It also reveals important potential links between housing and human performance and to generate the data on the same.
- There is a need for conducting further research in the topics like , building material, effect of environ-ment on building materials, building materials and indoor environment, building materials and human performance; both in a multi-disciplinary aspect and in an international context. Use of the experience from other researches is by that reason of great importance – both in order to inspire and to inform.
- Need is revealed for active research work in order to find fundamental understanding of physical factors and biological organisms – especially about the situation in residential building constructions combined with modern organic building materials and use.

3 Methodology

The main purpose of the study was to focus on organic building materials, which are being used from ancient times but have not been regarded as a matter of research, particularly for finding out what type of effect they have on the residents living inside the houses made up of these materials.

The research design, conceptual framework showing the relationship of variables and operational definitions of the terms used in the study are explained briefly. The sampling technique, selection and construction of the tool for the data collection and analysis of data are also described for the study.

This chapter presents the procedure adopted for conducting the present investigation in detail under the following heads:

3.1 Research design,
3.2 Conceptual framework of the study,
3.3 Variables under study,
3.4 Operational definitions,
3.5 Development of instrument,
3.6 Selection of sample,
3.7 Method of data collection,
3.8 Analysis of data.

3.1 Research Design

Exploratory cum experimental research design was selected to describe, to correlate and to measure effect of organic building materials on housing conditions and psychological behaviour of residents.

The exploratory research design was chosen as it describes, explores, records, analyzes and interprets conditions that exist. It involves some type of comparison or contrast and attempts to discover relationships between existing non-manipulated variables. It also describes, what will happen when certain variables are carefully controlled or manipulated (Kothari, 1990).

The experimental design was chosen to study environmental conditions of house and behaviour of residents. Its main purpose is to describe what will be the impact when certain variables are controlled. Its focus is also on relationships of variables (Singh, 2000). Experi-ments were conducted on a limited number of respondents for detailed analysis of housing conditions and their inter-relationship with performance of people living inside the houses made up of organic building materials.

3.2 Conceptual Framework of the Study

It is conceptualized that respondents' personal, family and situational variables have impact on the intervening variables i.e. their knowledge regarding the building materials, extent of use of organic building materials and problems faced during care and maintenance of home. The impact of these selected intervening variables was also seen directly on satisfaction and effect on health of residents. These intervening variables in turn affect the satisfaction of the respondents with regards to use of OBM. Further analysis was done to find out the impact of temperature and humidity inside the houses on health and human performance of the residents (Figure 3.1).

3.3 Variables under Study

It is certainly not possible, theoretical or otherwise to

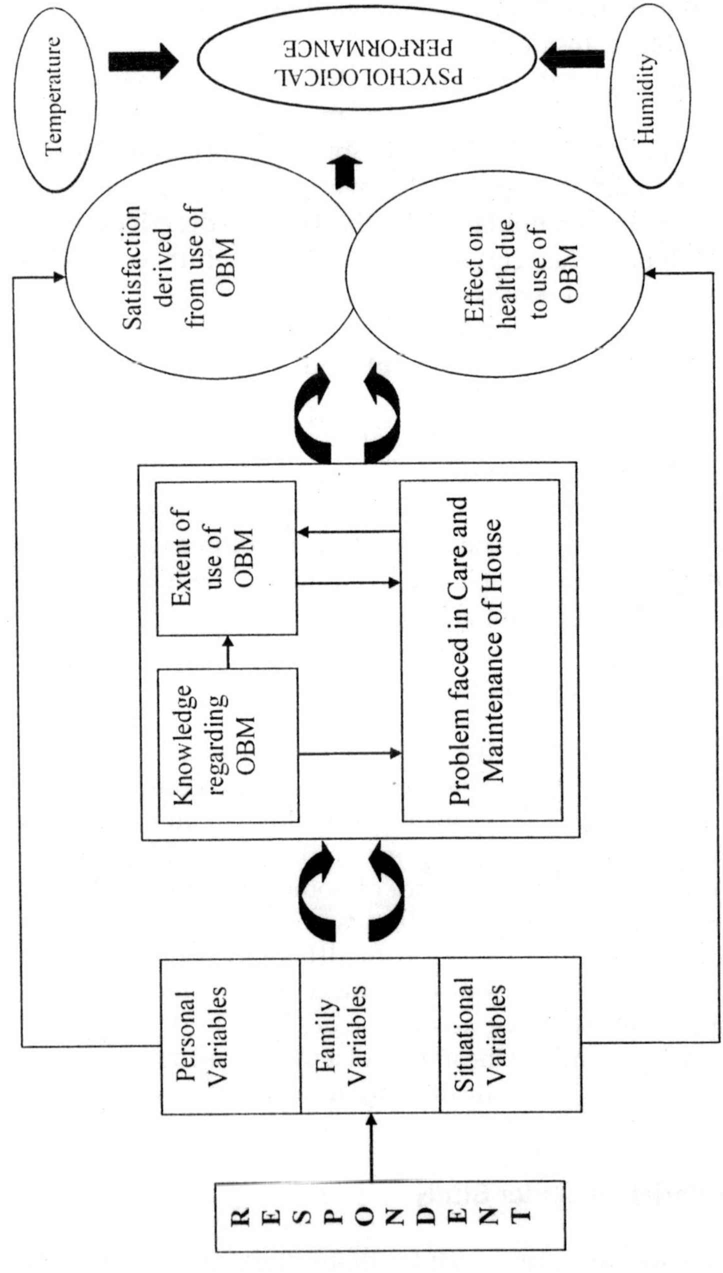

Figure 3. 1 : Conceptual Framework of the Study

postulate any definite cause effect relationship between any two variables, in particular, in a situation where a number of other factors influence behaviour of individuals to a most pronounced degree (Sharma, 1993).

There are several factors which rationalize the study. Hypothetical relationships of these variables for the study are presented here (Figure 3.2).

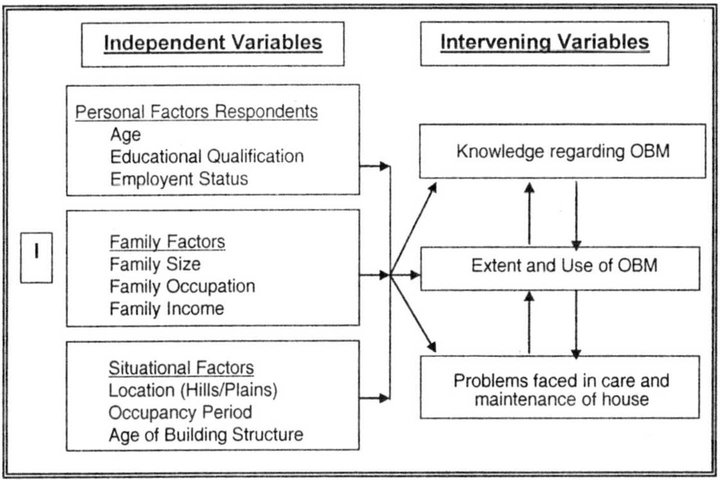

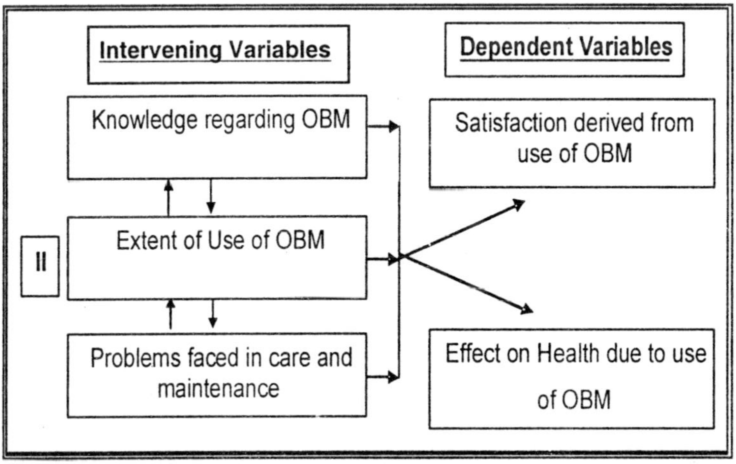

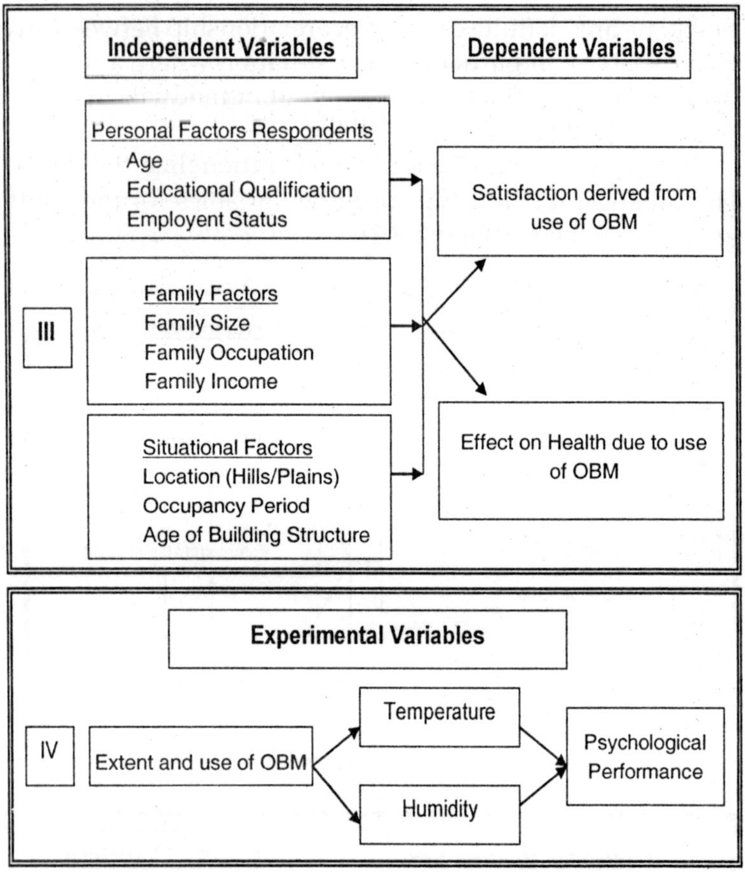

Figure 3.2 : Hypothetical Representation of Variables

Independent Variables

Variables not having any dependency over any other variable are independent variables. Independent variables selected for the present study are as follows:

1. Personal Variables

This category of independent variables includes age,

educational qualification and employment status of respondents.

(a) *Age of Respondent :* Age was found to be a factor influencing extent of involvement in various decisions (Agarwal, 1979; Kaur, 1983; Talwar, 1984; Sharma, 1993). Age was supposed to have an effect on intervening variables of the study. Therefore, it was selected as variable for the present study. It was recorded in complete chronological years.

(b) *Educational Qualification of Respondents:* Education is a very important factor which may influence level of knowledge, extent of use of various building materials and thus problems faced in care and maintenance of home. It has been observed that educational level is the factor which many times is responsible for participation in various decisions made in family (Sethi, 1982; Talwar, 1984; Agarwal, 1986 and Sharma, 1993). Therefore, this factor was undertaken for the study.

(c) *Employment Status of Respondents :* Employment status of respondent means gainful employment which generates monetary value further adding to living standard. This factor appears to be an important variable as it has a direct effect on intervening variables such as: the extent of use of materials to be used in home and method adopted for care and maintenance of home. It indirectly influences knowledge regarding organic building materials, as respondent interacts with various people at his/her workplace.

2. Family Variables

This category includes family size, occupation of head of family and income of family.

(a) Family Size

Family size reported to be associated with participation in different activities (Agarwal, 1989 and Sharma, 1993) and has an effect on dependent variables through participation in care and maintenance in the home. Therefore, it has been considered to be a variable for this study.

(b) Occupation of Head of Family

Mostly the occupation of head of family decides the type of house the family construct and the vicinity, too. The intervening variables such as knowledge regarding Organic Building Materials (OBM) of extent and use of OBM may be affected by the occupation of the head of the family.

(c) Family Income

Income of family affects the situational variables, as well as intervening variables. Therefore, it was found to be an important variable to be selected for the study. It was recorded as sum of monthly income in rupees earned by all members of the family.

3. Situational Variables

This category includes location of house, occupancy period and age of building structure.

(a) Location of House

Locality and geographic factors all together influence conditions of house, intervening variables and also immediate environment to be lived in it. Therefore, location of house in terms of hills and plains was noted.

(b) Occupancy Period

The factor was supposed to be important, because the effects of building materials on the health of the residents can be determined on repeated exposure in the houses. Therefore, it was included as a situational variable for purpose of the present study.

(c) Age of Building Structure

Type of building materials used in construction have a tendency to influence various factors like existing living conditions and problems faced during care and maintenance of house thus having an effect on satisfaction derived from use of organic building materials, effect on health as well as performance of people residing in it. Therefore, this variable was found to be an important factor and was measured in terms of number of years completed since its construction.

Intervening Variables

These are the variables which connect independent and dependent variables by having a relationship with the both directly and/or indirectly thus, establishing cause-effect relationships with other variables. Intervening variables taken up for the study are knowledge regarding OBM, extent of use of OBM and problems faced in care and maintenance of house (Figure 3.2).

1. Knowledge Regarding OBM

A dichotomous explanation of knowledge was given by Cohen and Squire (1980); it can be declarative or proce-dural. Declarative knowledge is explicit and accessible to conscious awareness, it can be declared, i.e. brought to mind, either verbally or non-verbally, and includes both episodic knowledge (specific time and place events), as well as semantic knowledge (facts and general information). By way of contrast, procedural knowledge is defined as being implicit and accessible only by engaging in the skills or operations in which that knowledge is fixed. This variable has its importance in terms of influencing extent of use of OBM and problems faced in care and maintenance of house directly and dependent variables indirectly. For the purpose of the study it includes basic knowledge regarding OBM used in residential constructions, their extent of familiarity, proper use and effect on health.

2. Extent of Use of OBM

It was postulated that extent of use of any OBM creates a physical as well as psychological environment within a house which do have an effect on problems faced in care and maintenance of house, satisfaction derived from their use, health of people residing in the house and their performance of various tasks.

3. Problems Faced in Care and Maintenance of House

It was assumed as prerequisite that care and maintenance of house against wear and tear requires time, energy as well as money. They create a pressure on the residents which in turn affect the satisfaction derived from use of OBM, effect on health of the residents and performance of the residents.

Dependent Variables

These are the variables which are related to independent variables. As the name suggests they have certain kind of dependency over other factors. Dependent variables taken for the study are satisfaction derived from use of OBM, effect of these materials on the health and human performance of residents in their homes. These are described as under:

1. Satisfaction Derived from use of OBM

Satisfaction here means feeling of atonement or adequacy

from use after using organic building materials in residential constructions. This variable is likely to affect of intervening variables such as problems faced during care and maintenance of the houses. This variable was measured by using a satisfaction scale developed for the purpose.

2. Effect on Health due to use of OBM

Health is not merely a state of physical conditions of a body but it is a physiological, psychological and sociological well-being. In the present study it is defined as physiological symptoms of illness or syndrome, perceived as an effect of organic building materials by the residents.

3. Psychological Performance

Human performance analyzes individual differences generally on basis of psychological performance, physiological performance and physical performance (Mathews *et al.* 2000). For the purpose of the study it was considered to be taken as combination of cognitive performance, sensory motor system and vigilance/attention/concentration abilities of the respondent.

3.4 Operational Definitions

Following are certain concepts used in the study. They are operationally defined as under:

Organic Building Materials (OBM)

Organic Building Materials are engineering materials, made by a mixture of different hydrocarbons sometimes together with sulphur, nitrogen and oxygen derivatives, used in residential constructions. Organic materials used on or in buildings can be classified according to their use. They include liquid coatings (paints), plastics, sealants, and roofing materials. Wood, although often placed in a separate category, is really an organic building material (Ashton, 1969). The organic substances contain the element carbon (and usually hydrogen) as a key part of their structure. All living animals and plants are organic.

Care and Maintenance of House

House needs continuous protection against wear and tear, depreciation, etc. to support its original living conditions. It includes human and non-human resources to be involved simultaneously. Data for the study includes person, time and frequency of cleaning involved, cost and frequency of repair, marketing sources of OBM during construction and renovation, techniques to withstand accidents, defective symptoms or problems encountered in home.

Health Problems Perceived

For the purpose of the study it refers to physiological symptoms of illness or syndrome, perceived as an effect of organic building materials by the residents. Data recorded for the variable are minor health symptoms, their frequency of occurrence and seriousness of building related syndrome.

Knowledge Regarding OBM

Knowledge means awareness or familiarity, person's range of information and understanding of a particular subject (Oxford Dictionary, 1994). For the present study data were recorded by using a knowledge scale on various aspects of organic building materials.

Satisfaction Regarding OBM

It is a feeling of adequacy derived after use of anything. For the study it was ascertained by using a self prepared satisfaction scale on different aspects viz. cost, care and maintenance, function/purpose, safety and no health effects of OBM.

Human Performance

Acquisition of doing anything to carry out life processes is known to be performance. It can be learned or natural. Mental performance, physiological performance, physical performance and individual differences, help in analyzing human performance. In this study data are recorded by a combination of tests/equipments for short-term memory, attention/concentration, work and fatigue, temperature and humidity.

3.5 Development of Instrument

(A) Selection of Tool

Pre-coded interview schedule (Annexure 1) was used as an instrument for collecting data due to following reasons:

1. To ensure completely filled in data sheets,
2. To safeguard against non-return of the data sheets,
3. To establish rapport in order to elicit correct response and to clarify the issues.

(B) Construction of Tool

An interview schedule having descriptive statements, observation charts and experiment sheets was developed to collect subjective as well as experimental data during face to face interview with residents. The instrument consisted of sections as following:

Section I : It comprised of questions regarding general information, care and maintenance of house, health problems as perceived by residents, knowledge scale regarding OBM and satisfaction scale to assess satisfaction derived from use of OBM.

Section II : This section was having observation cum interview sheet. It dealt with observation chart of materials used in residential construction. It also included a checklist of defective symptoms as observed in home given by Bowyer in 1973.

Section III : It contained experiment sheets to record and judge cognition, sensory motor abilities and attention/concentration of respondents. It also comprised of experiment sheet to record temperature and humidity as environmental factors.

(C) Development of Knowledge Test

Knowledge tests used in the measurements of level of knowledge have proved to be useful in a variety of research problems. The objective of determining level of knowledge of the respondents requires a standardized knowledge test. For quantitative measurements the concept of scaling method is mostly used. The level of knowledge of the respondents is determined in terms of whether they possess good, medium or low knowledge. This is measured by giving scores to answers for each item in the test and by addition of the scores for each respondent.

To measure the level of knowledge of the respondents regarding quality of environment, an attempt has been made to develop a knowledge test in view of the fact that it plays an important role in achieving and maintaining quality of the environment in the residential constructions.

Construction and Standardization of the Test

The content of the test comprised of questions called items. The most important factor considered in collecting the items for the knowledge test was to include the various aspects of OBM like, their origin, use, constituents, utility, physiological and psychological effect and so on.

The items were collected from the literature reviewed. Special care was taken to include relevant information. Following criteria were kept in mind while selecting the items for the test:

(1) The statement should be as simple as possible,
(2) They should be clear, brief and related to the problem.

The items collected for constructing the knowledge test were all framed in the simple statement with objective type answers so that the respondents could respond to them either positively or negatively. The selection of the items were done keeping in mind the fact that it should differentiate the well informed respondents from the poorly informed respondents and should have a certain difficulty value and that it should promote thinking of the respondents. One hundred and twenty possible and relevant items were framed to constitute the initial test.

Content Validity of the Knowledge Test

The aim was to develop a scale that would satisfy content validity. The validity of scale concerns with what the scale measures and how well it does so. The content validity assesses the relevance of the scale to the stated purpose. Content validation is basically judgmental and intuitive. It can be determined by using a panel of persons who shall judge how well the measuring instrument meets the standards.

Content validity refers to degree to which test actually measures, or is specially related to traits for which it was designed. It is determined by using a panel of persons who judge its adequacy and how well the measuring instrument meets standards (Helmstadter, 1964). Therefore, the set of carefully selected one hundred and twenty items related to the topic was given to a panel of twelve judges consisting of experts in the field from OBM Division in C.B.R.I., Roorki; Department of Civil Engineering, Department of Psychology and Department of Home Management in The Maharaja Sayaji Rao University of Baroda; whereas Department of Civil Engineering, Department of Home Science Extension, Department of Family Resource Management and Directorate of Research in G.B. Pant University of Agriculture and Technology, Pantnagar. The judges were requested to sort out the statements in terms of its correctness or incorrectness. This was felt necessary so that the investigator could make sure of herself in discriminating correct or incorrect statements. They were also requested to indicate their judgment on clarity and applicability of the statements. All the responses of the judges were coded and tabulated and analyzed for each statement. The screening of the items was done on the basis of the following criteria:

(1) The statement classified as 'clear' by more than seventy five per cent of the judges was retained in the scale.
(2) The scale which was reported as 'applicable' by more than seventy five per cent of judges was included in the test.

Very few statements which were indicated as 'ambiguous', but were very much applicable to the study were made more clear and approved by judges after modifications. After the analysis of the judgment given by the panel of experts, eight statements which were not meeting the above criteria were eliminated from the scale. Thus, out of the original set of one hundred and twenty items, one hundred and twelve items which fulfilled the above criteria were included in the final (Annexure 1).

Pre-Testing of the Scale

The schedule so developed was pre-tested on 33 randomly selected residents of a non-sampled group. A pilot study was done to see the feasibility and clarity of the interview schedule and to establish the reliability of knowledge test. Few changes were incorporated in the interview schedule and the tool for data collection was finalized.

Item Analysis of the Knowledge Test

The knowledge test was analyzed quantitatively by doing item analysis to increase validity and reliability of the test. Item analysis was done to eliminate inconsistency of the items. The respondents were asked to answer the items in dichotomous categories i.e. whether the statement is 'correct' or 'incorrect'. Both correct and incorrect statements were included for counter checking. Almost equal number of positive and negative statements was included in the scale. All the right answers were given a score of '2' and wrong answers were given a score of '1'. These scores helped to determine the level of knowledge of the respondents. There was thus possibility of a respondent scoring maximum of 224 points for all right answers and 112 points for all wrong answers in the knowledge test. After adding the scores obtained by the 33 respondents in a pilot study, the scores were arranged from highest to the lowest in magnitude. The statements for the final test were retained on the basis of the typical item analysis of the knowledge test by calculating 't values' and arranging them in descending order. One hundred and two statements with higher 't-values' were included for the final test.

Reliability Coefficient of the Knowledge Test

Split half technique was adopted to determine the reliability coefficient of the test. According to this method of calculating reliability, the whole scale was divided into two halves using odd numbered items for one half and even numbered items for the other half. The scores of the subjects for odd numbered and even numbered items were summed and each of the two sets was treated as separate scale. The respondent who scored high on the odd items should score high on the even items as well, if empirical errors have been kept to a minimum and the same applies in case of low scores also. The coefficient of correlation 'r' between odd and even scores of thirty respondents was computed by using Pearson's Product Moment Correlation Coefficient (Gupta, 1981). The correlation coefficient of the half test derived was 0.436. From the self correlation of two halves of the test, the reliability coefficient of the whole test was estimated by using the Spearman Brown Prophecy Formula (Garrett, 1979). The reliability of the knowledge test thus calculated was 0.607.

The index of reliability 'r' measures the trustworthiness of the test scores by showing how well obtained scores agree with their theoretically true counterparts. The index of reliability is also taken as a measure of validity. The formula given by Garrett in 1979 was used to calculate the index of reliability. By using the formula, the index of reliability of the knowledge test was found 0.779. This means, 0.779 is the highest correlation of which this test is capable, since it represents the relationship between obtained test scores and true test scores in the same function.

(D) Development of Satisfaction Scale to Assess Satisfaction Derived from use of OBM in Residential Constructions

A three point Likert type scale was developed to assess satisfaction derived from use of OBM in residential constructions. Likert scale is one which consists of a number of statements that express either a favourable or unfavourable degree towards a given object to which the respondent is asked to react (Kothari, 1990). Various items, on basis of literature reviewed and survey done were collected under five categories namely cost, care and maintenance, function/ purpose, safety and health regarding OBM.

Items relevant to above cited five categories were formulated. The items were brief, clear and related to the study. The satisfaction scale initially had forty statements.

Construction, Standardization and Content Validity of the Satisfaction Scale

The scale with forty statements under five categories to assess satisfaction level regarding use of OBM was given to same panel of judges as for validation of the knowledge scale. The judges were requested to check and score each statement on a six point score sheet (Annexure 2). Their evaluation was requested to be based on the objectives of the study and following criteria were adopted for final inclusion of statement in the scale:

(1) Items on which there was agreement of seventy per cent or more judges with regards to clarity of the statement.
(2) Those items on which seventy per cent or more judges had considered them relevant to the information to be elicited.

After testing its validity the scale had the forty statements.

Pre-Testing of the Scale

A pilot study on 33 respondents from Rudrapur block of Udham Singh Nagar district in Uttaranchal was conducted. Test-Rest method was applied to evaluate internal consistency of the scale. The scale was repeated after a gap of forty five days.

Reliability Coefficient of the Satisfaction Scale

Reliability refers to the accuracy in terms of consistency and stability of measurement by a test (Anastasi, 1982). The reliability varies from zero to one, having the former value when the measurement involves nothing but error and reading the latter value only when there is no variable error at all in the measurement. The weighted score for each item in the first test and in the re-test for all respondents was summed up. The total scores of thirty three respondents were arranged in descending order. Each item was analyzed to determine how effectively it helps to differentiate between the high and the low scores. The 't' value for each item was computed to find out the discriminating power of each item. Only those items which showed a significant difference between high and low scorers were retained for the final scale. Out of forty statements only thirty six statements were included for the final scale after item analysis. To establish reliability of the scale coefficient of correlation was computed by using Pearson's Product Moment Correlation Coefficient (Gupta, 1981). The correlation coefficient of the test derived was 0.692. By using the formula of the index of reliability of the satisfaction test was found 0.904. This means, 0.904 is the highest correlation of which this test is capable.

3.6 Selection of Sample

(A) Selection of Locale

Uttaranchal State is divided into hill areas and plain (tarai and bhabar regions) areas. The study was conducted in Nainital district from hill areas and Udham Singh Nagar district in plain areas (Plate 3.1). To ignore biasedness in results due to different geographical factors in the state the residential buildings in hill as well as plain region were selected. The selection of districts provided combination of residential buildings having organic building materials in

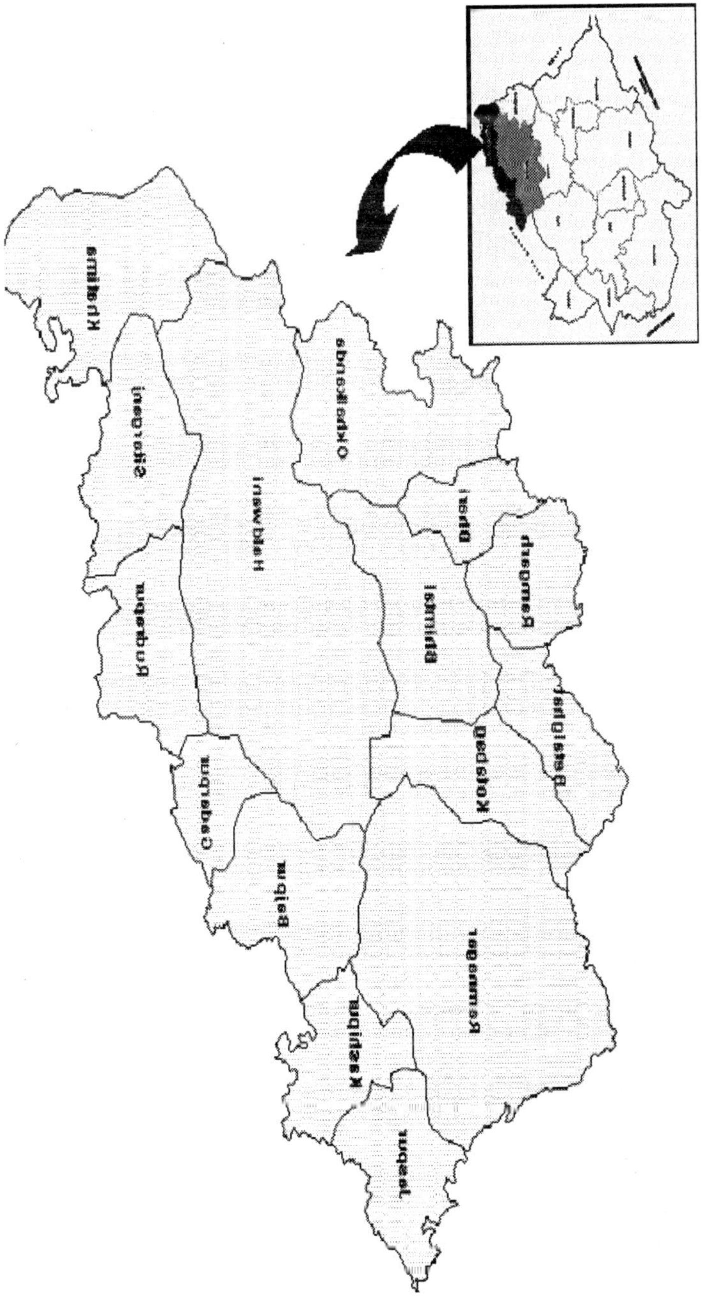

Plate 3.1 : Development Blocks of District Nainital and Udham Singh Nagar

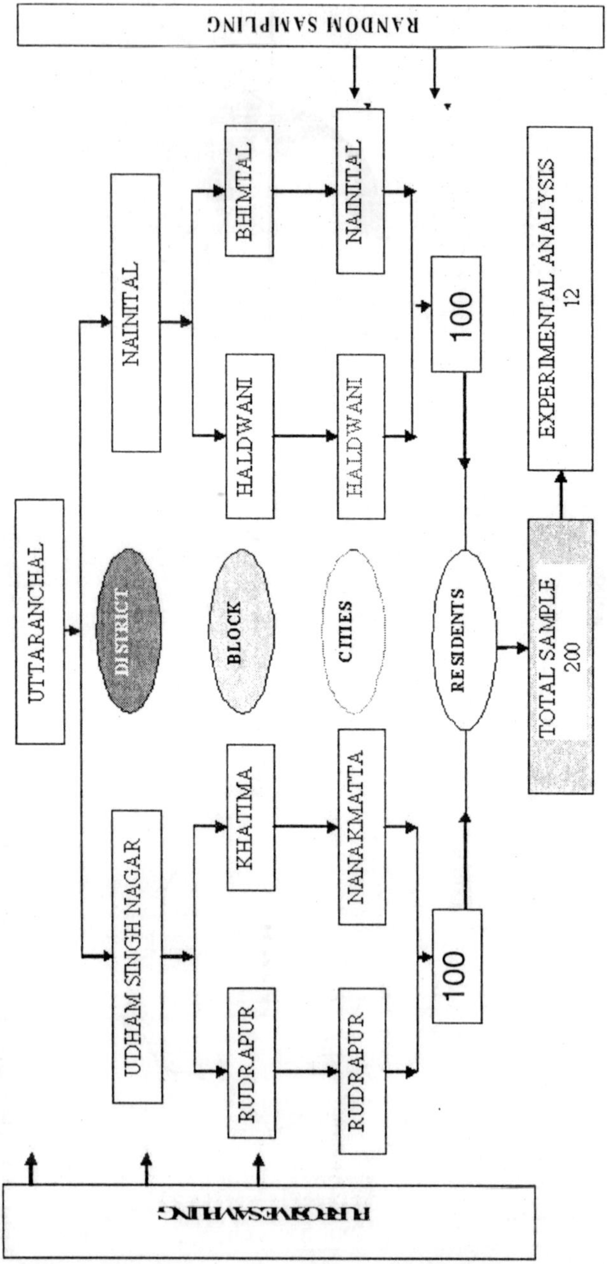

Figure 3.3 : Schematic Representation of Sampling Design

different environmental conditions; and further no study of its kind has been carried out in the area.

(B) Sampling Design

Multi-stage purposive-cum-random sampling design is one where researcher moves step by step to select sample from population sometimes purposively and sometimes randomly to fulfil objectives of the research. To select state, districts and blocks purposive sampling was adopted and random sampling design was found to be appropriate to select residential buildings.

(C) Selection of Sample

For selection of sample Department of Statistics in Nainital and Udham Singh Nagar districts were contacted. The list of primary census data for blocks, cities and occupied residential houses served as a basis to select the sample of 200 residential houses. It is very much clear from the Figure 3.3.

3.7 Method of Data Collection

Phase I: Descriptive Work

It was assumed that to record information in the interview schedule personal interview method is appropriate. Therefore, data were gathered by personally contacting each respondent. A visit was made to each of the selected place prior to data collection in order to establish a rapport with the respondents. Unit of enquiry was residential building for investigation. Key informants chosen were house-wives assuming that they remain in their houses for longer hours. They are the ones who are involved in care and maintenance of their houses thus has better knowledge of various aspects

Table 3.1 : Equipments/Methods used to Record Different Parameters of the Study

Sl. No.	*Parameter*		*Equipment/Method*
1.	Inventory of OBM	-	Interview - Observation
2.	Extent of use	-	Interview - Observation
3.	Problem experienced in care and maintenance	-	Check list of defective symptoms & problems.
4.	Perceived health problems	-	Health problem Scale
5.	Knowledge level regarding OBM	-	Knowledge Scale
6.	Satisfaction level of residents regarding OBM use.	-	Satisfaction Scale
7.	Human performance		
	(a) Short-term memory		Cognition test by Berglund *et al.*, 1987 Perterson *et al.*, 1959 Ost *et al.*, 1969 (Annexure 2)
	(b) Attention		Vigilance test by Dashiell, 1931; Kuppuswamy, 1953; Berglund *et al.*, 1987. (Annexure 3)
	(c) Fatigue (mental)		Sensory-motor test by Dashiell, 1931 Kuppuswamy, 1953. (Annexure 4)
8.	Environmental parameters		
	(a) Temperature indoors	-	Digital thermo-hygro clock (Plate-3.2)
	(b) Temperature outdoors	-	Secondary data
	(c) Humidity indoors	-	Digital thermo-hygro clock (Plate-3.2)
	(d) Humidity outdoors	-	Secondary data

of their houses. Family members were also interviewed for few questions to supplement and cross check the information provided by the respondents. Respondents were interviewed in Hindi as it is local language and to maintain consistency while interviewing.

Phase II: Experimental Work

To assess level of human performance in the selected residential buildings with OBM constructions, it was felt necessary to conduct experiments on certain psychological aspects and indoor environment of the residents, in terms of :

Plate 3.2 : Thermo Hygro Clock Used to Record Environmental Parameters of the Study

- Short-term Memory,
- Work and Fatigue,
- Attention/Concentration
- Temperature,
- Humidity.

The above parameters were recorded with standar-dized test and equipments as mentioned in Table 3.1. The data were collected during period of June 2004 to April 2005. For various parameters of the study following equipments/methods were adopted to collect data:

3.8 Analysis of Data

Descriptive as well as relational statistics were used to analyze the data in the study. The data were categorized, tabulated and presented in frequencies, percentages, mean, standard deviation for analyzing various information, the standard statistical analysis was done to test the hypothesis of the study.

(A) Categorization

The variables of the study were categorized for purpose of tabulation and analysis. A detailed description of categorization is as under:

1. Age

Age was measured in number of complete years by the respondents at time of the interview. It was categorized on equal interval basis as:

Categories

Young	:	20-30 years
Middle	:	31-40 years
Old	:	41-50 years
Very Old	:	above 51 years

2. Educational Qualification

Education here referred to reading and writing abilities as well as formal education attained by the residents. It was divided into following categories:

Categories

Illiterate	:	not having formal education
Low level	:	up to high school
Middle level	:	intermediate
High level	:	degree or diploma

3. Employment Status

It is the status of the respondent with reference to gainful employment. It was divided in two categories:

Categories

Employed	:	gainfully employed outside home
Unemployed	:	not employed outside home

4. Family Size

Family size refers to the total number of members in the family consisting of husband, wife, children and other dependents residing under same roof. It did not include the children who left the house after marriage or expired. The family size was categorized as:

Categories

Small	:	less than 5 members
Medium	:	5 to 10 members
Large	:	more than 10 members

5. Occupational Status

It refers to family's source of income of the family. It was categorized into following categories:

Categories

Business	:	personal means of livelihood
Service	:	earning wages from any organization
Agriculture	:	earning from cultivation in fields

6. Family Income

Family income refers to monthly income accrued from various sources of respondent's family such as farm produce, service, business, dairypoultry and other income generating activities. The family income ranges were made according to Taxation Enquiry Committee, 1991: Govt. of India Publication.

Categories

Low income level	:	upto Rs. 1700 per month
Medium income level	:	Rs. 1701-4200 per month
Medium high income level	:	Rs. 4201-8400 per month
High income level	:	Rs. 8401 per month and above

7. Location of Residence

Immediate environment of the house where it is situated is known to be locality. It was operationalized for the study as:

Categories

Hills
Plains

8. Age of Housing Structure

Period of residence from the date it was built to the present point of time for interview was recorded as age of the housing structure and it was categorized into:

Categories

Less than 5 years
6-10 years
More than 11 years

9. Occupancy Period

Period of residency from the date they were living in the residence to the present point of time for interview was taken as occupancy period. It was categorized into following three categories:

Categories

Less than 5 years
6 10 years
More than 11 years

10. Knowledge Regarding OBM

It was measured by means of standardized knowledge test and was described in terms of low, medium or high level of knowledge on the basis of scores obtained by the respondents. The possible categories of scores were as following:

Categories	Range of Score
Low knowledge	102-135
Medium knowledge	136-170
High knowledge	171-204

11. Satisfaction Derived from use of OBM

It is the feeling of atonement derived after use of OBM in the residents by the respondents. It was recorded by using a self developed satisfaction scale. The possible categories of the level of satisfaction derived by the respondents after use of OBM in their houses were as following:

Categories	Range of Score
Highly satisfactory	85-108
Satisfactory	61-84
Not satisfactory	36-60

12. Effect on Health

Effect on health was taken as per the feeling of physical problems perceived by the residents as an effect of OBM in their residences. The health problems were categorized as:

Extent of Health Problems	Range of Score
High	49-63
Moderate	35-48
Low	21-34

(B) Statistical Treatment of the Data

The data were statistically analyzed employing descriptive as well as relational statistics for drawing of inferences:

Descriptive Statistics: The data were presented in percentages, measures of central tendency (mean) and measures of dispersion (Standard Deviation) for analyzing the information.

Relational Statistics: Relational statistics was applied to test relationship between selected independent variables with dependent variables of the study. Karl Pearson product movement coefficient of correlation, t-test, regression analysis and Analysis of Variance (ANOVA) were employed to test the hypothesis formulated for the present study.

4 Results and Discussion

Findings of the research work on the organic building materials are described and discussed in this chapter. To ignore biasedness in results due to different geographical factors in the state the residential buildings in hill as well as plain region were selected and cumulative results are presented.

The findings are presented in composite frequency and percentage summary tables. These are followed by statistical applications for testing the hypotheses. Important views about the findings are discussed at the end of the chapter in order to review, correlate and justify the results. This is done under light of few studies of other researchers and supported by some other facts. The results are summarized as per the objectives of the study under following sections:

4.1 Description of the respondents and their houses
4.2 Organic Building Materials
4.3 Experimental Results

- Checklist of defective symptoms in the houses
- Short-term memory
- Work and Fatigue
- Attention/Concentration
- Temperature
- Humidity

4.4 Testing of Hypotheses

SECTION: 4.1

DESCRIPTION OF THE RESPONDENTS AND THEIR HOUSES

This section includes personal characteristics of the respondents, their family characteristics, general living habits and general information of their houses. The home-makers were the key respondents for the study.

1. Personal Profile of the Respondents

Personal profile of the respondents was comprised of age, educational qualification and employment status. (Table 4.1)

Table 4.1: Personal Profile of the Respondents (n = 200)

S. No. Characteristics	*Respondents*	
	Frequency	*Percentage*
1. *Age (years)*		
20-30	69	34.50
31-40	80	40.00
41-50	34	17.00
Above 51	17	8.50
Mean Age (Years)		36.20
S.D.		+9.16
2. *Educational Qualification Illiterate*	–	00.00
Low Level : Can read and write	30	15.00
High School	24	12.00
Middle Level : Intermediate	67	33.50
High Level : Degree or Diploma	79	39.50
3. *Employment Status*		
Employed	24	12.00
Unemployed	176	88.00

Mean age of the respondents was 36.20 years. Therefore,

little less than half i.e. 40 per cent of the respondents were found to be in the age group of 31-40 years. Their age differed by a standard deviation (S.D.) of + 9.16 years. (Figure 4.1)

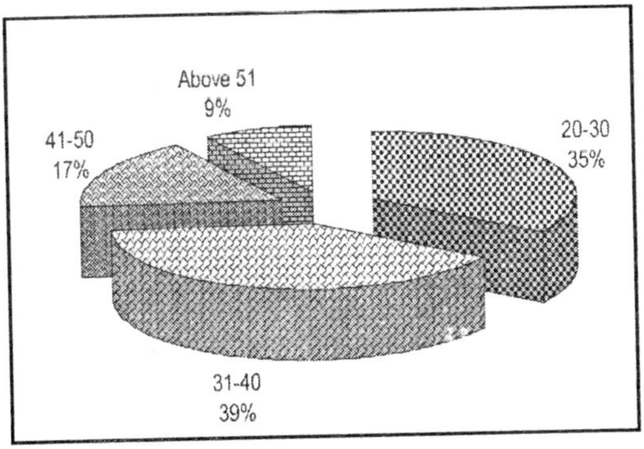

Figure 4.1 : Personal Profile of the Respondents according to their Age (years)

About one-third of the respondents (39.50 per cent) were highly qualified having a degree or diploma and none of them was illiterate. Less than one-third of the respondents (27.00 per cent) were having a low level of educational qualification. (Figure 4.2)

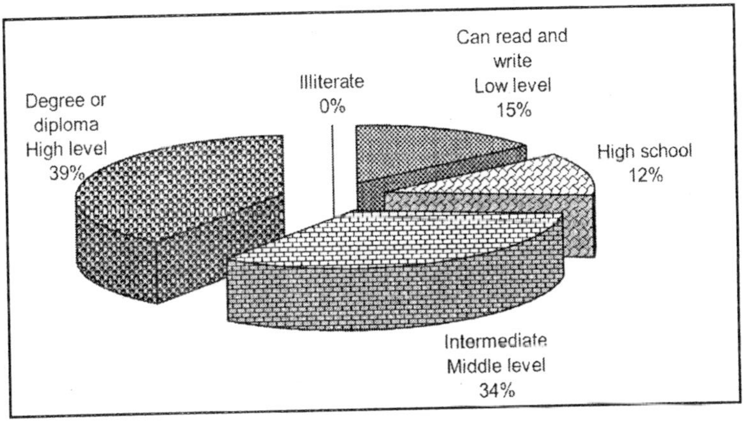

Figure 4.2: Personal Profile of the Respondents according to their Educational Qualification

About more than three-fourth of the respondents were unemployed (88 per cent). They were house-wives, taking care of their families and spending most of the time indoors. (Figure 4.3)

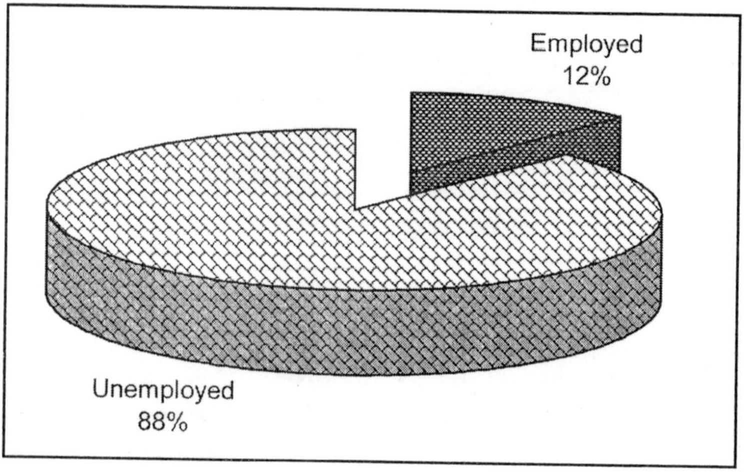

Figure 4.3 : Personal Profile of the Respondents according to their Employment Status

There is no control on allocation of housing. The social scientist investigates differences in health circumstances that actually do exist in the population. By asking a range of questions concerning the respondents' social, demographic, environmental and other circumstances, the social scientist analytically remove all other factors that might be related to variations in health experiences (Burridge *et al.*, 1993).

2. Demographic Profile of the Respondents

Occupational status and monthly income of the family were considered for demographic profile of the selected respondents.

Among the selected families more than a half of the families (67.50 per cent) were having a medium size of the families consisting of 5-10 family members. Some of the families (13.50 per cent) reported large family of more than 10 family members. (Figure 4.4)

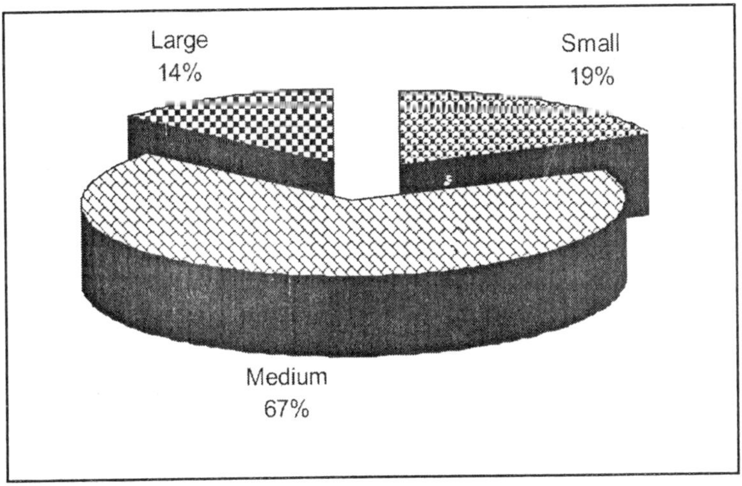

Figure 4.4 : Demographic Profile of the Respondents according to their Family Size

About half (51.50 per cent) of the respondents' families were having service as means of their income and a little less than half (42.50 per cent) of the families were generating their income from business, but a few of them (5.50 per cent) earned money from agriculture. (Figure 4.5)

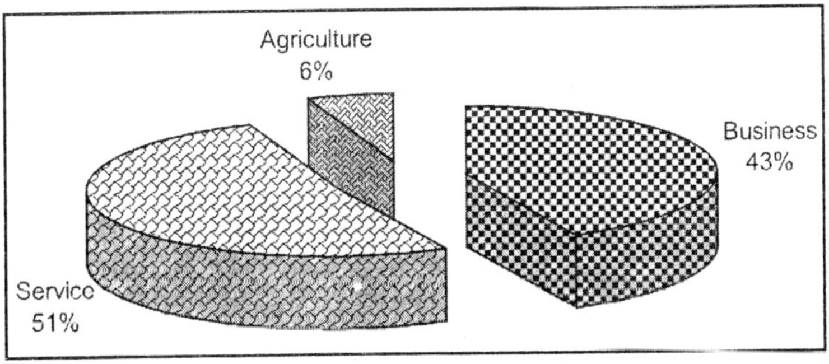

Figure 4.5: Demographic Profile of the Respondents according to their Occupational Status

The respondents were having family income of about Rs. 9,400 with a standard difference of ± Rs. 5826.92. Forty per cent of them belonged to medium high level of monthly income. (Figure 4.6)

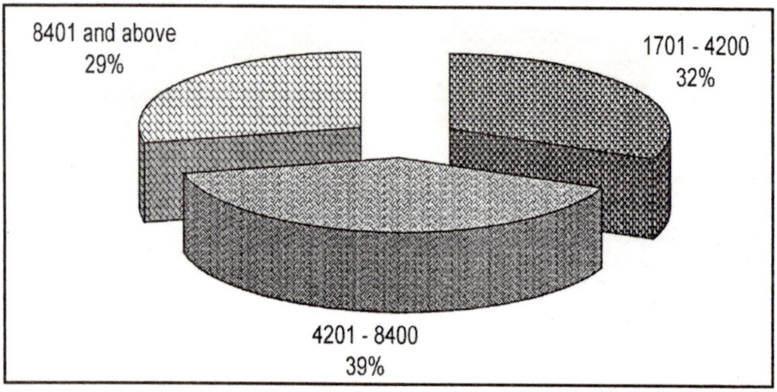

Figure 4.6 : Demographic Profile of the Respondents according to their Monthly Income (Rupees)

Thus medium size service class families were prominent with medium high income group.

Table 4.2: Demographic Profile of the Respondents (n = 200)

S. No.	*Characteristics*		*Respondents*	
			Frequency	*Percentage*
1.	*Family Size*			
	Small		38	19.00
	Medium		135	67.50
	Large		27	13.50
2.	*Occupational Status**			
	Business		85	42.50
	Service		103	51.50
	Agriculture		11	5.50
3	*Monthly Income***			
	Medium	: 1701-4200	63	31.50
	Medium High	: 4201-8400	80	40.00
	High	: 8401 and above	57	28.50
	Mean Income			9400
	S.D.			± 5826.92

* Figures shows multiple responses. ** Taxation Inquiry Committee, 1991

3. General Information about the Houses of the Respondents

For the purpose of the study it was found important to record information about general conditions of the selected houses therefore location of the house, type of house, age of building structure and occupancy period was recorded. Therefore, fifty per cent selected respondents were from hill areas and fifty per cent were from plains.

Table 4.3 : General Information about the Houses of the Respondents (n = 200)

S. No.	Characteristics	Respondents	
		Frequency	*Percentage*
1.	*Location of House*		
	Hills	100	50.00
	Plains	100	50.00
2.	*Type of House*		
	Kachcha	—	—
	Pucca	189	94.50
	Semi-*pucca*	5	2.50
	Wooden	6	3.00
3.	*Age of Building Structure (years)*		
	Less than 5	—	—
	6-10	57	28.50
	More than 11	143	72.50
4	Occupancy Period (years)		
	Less than 5	—	—
	6-10	163	81.50
	More than 11	37	18.50

Most of the houses (94.50 percent) were *pucca* houses built with stone, bricks or any building material which is durable whereas, a very few of them were built as semi- *pucca* (2.50 per cent) and wooden (3 per cent). Through many generations of use, people have found ways of getting around some of the limitations of naturally occurring organic construction materials. In addition to improving natural materials, technologies have developed many synthetic polymers, which are important in current constructions (Merritt, 1986) and make the houses pucca. (Plate 4.1 and Plate 4.2).

Plate 4.1: A Modern Wooden House (*Pucca*)

Plate 4.2 : A Traditional Thatched House (*Kachcha*)

Among the selected residences about three-fourth of the houses (72.50 per cent) were built more than ten years ago and some of them were built between 5-10 years (28.50 per cent) ago.

Among the selected respondents most of them (81.50 per cent) were living in the selected houses for more than ten years and some of them were residing for 5-10 years (18.50 per cent).

From the Table 4.3 it is evident that most of the houses were *pucca* having built before more than eleven years and the respondents were residing in them for about 6-10 years which is enough time to find out relationship of building materials with the health, performance and environmental factors.

4. General Living Habits of the Respondents

Cecere *et al.*, (1998) reported that environmental and demographic risk factors are associated with the type of roof, presence of cracks in the walls and number of people living in the house. Thus general living habits like type of fuel used, numbers of smokers and period of occupancy per day was recorded.

Most of the selected families were using LPG (91.50 per cent) as a fuel for cooking and about one-third of them were using electricity (35.50 per cent) as a fuel for lighting, cooking as well as heating.

Eighty per cent of the respondents were not having any smoker in their families who smoked in the houses.

House wives were the member of families spending most of the time in their houses. Most of them were spending 19-24 hours (80 per cent), some of them were spending 13-18 hours (17.50 per cent) and very few of them were spending 6-12 hours (2.50 per cent) in their houses. Townsend *et al.* in 1988 also recommended that 'Hosing conditions are associated with health status in a variety of ways'. The conditions were found to be very much suitable to assess effect of OBM on the residents.

Table 4.4 : General Living Habits of the Respondents (n = 200)

S.No. Characteristics	Respondents	
	Frequency	Percentage
1. *Type of Fuel Used**		
Wood and Dung Cakes	—	—
Kerosene	6	3.00
LPG	183	91.50
Electricity	71	
2. *Smoker* in *House*		
Yes	40	20.00
No	160	80.00
3. *Period of Occupancy per Day*		
Less than 6 hours	—	—
7-12 hours	5	2.50
13-18 hours	35	17.50
19-24 hours	160	80.00

* Figures show multiple responses.

SECTION: 4.2

ORGANIC BUILDING MATERIALS

This section includes information about various organic building materials and their availability, throwing a light on extent of use of various organic building materials in homes and also on their purposes for using them. It reveals results of aspects of care and maintenance of the homes and problems perceived/experienced by the residents during care and maintenance and also deals with health problems/ symptoms/syndromes perceived as an effect of organic building material in the homes. The section also discusses level of knowledge regarding OBM and satisfaction derived after using the OBM on various parameters by the respondents.

5. Building Materials and their Sources

Source of building can be defined as the outlet of building materials from where the consumers could buy construction materials for construction and renovation purposes in their houses. The sources were categorized into three; local market, district market and market of the other state out side the native state. After that respondents were asked to report the sources from which the materials were bought by them. (Table 4.5)

Table 4.5: Building Materials and Their Sources (n = 200)

S.No. Building Materials	*Respondents*	
	Frequency	*Percentage*
1. *Masonry*		
From local market	72	36.00
Within the district	126	63.00
From other state	12	6.00
2. *Metals*		
From local market	15	7.50
Within the district	129	64.50
From other state	56	28.00
3. *Wood/Plastic/Glass*		
From local market	137	68.50
Within the district	13	6.50
From other state	50	25.00
4. *Roofing/Sealant/Adhesive*		
From local market	118	59.00
Within the district	78	39.00
From other state	4	2.00
5. *Protective/Decorative Finishes*		
From local market	3	1.50
Within the district	190	95.00
From other state	7	3.50
6 *Reinforcement/Basic*		
From local market	25	12.50
Within the district	78	39.00
From other state	97	48.50

* Figures show multiple responses.

About more than a half of the respondents reported that they got building materials for the masonry (63.00 per cent) and metals (64.50 per cent) from district market. Whereas, it was also reported that a large number of the respondents (95.00 per cent) preferred to buy protective/decorative finishes from district market. Just about a half of the respondents got materials like wood/plastic/glass (68.50 per cent) and roofing/sealant/adhesive (59.00 per cent) in the local market. Building materials for reinforcement/basic material were available in the local market, district market as well as the markets of the state and the respondents bought them as per their feasibility and convenience.

It was observed that the materials for roofing/sealants/adhesives were available in the local market but other building materials were available within the district market and the materials for reinforcement/basic structure was found in out of state markets.

6. Finishes/Techniques used for Selected Factors Causing Damage to the Houses

Weathering is a process of disintegration of building structure as a result of environmental forces; moisture, gases, sunlight, humidity, temperature, etc. Besides, environmental forces some environmental hazards like earthquakes and factors of infestation like termite also affect durability of the building materials thus the building structure. The houses were categorized into various areas on the basis of their utility in the home then respondents were asked to report the type of finishes used specifically to withstand the hazards. Data observed in Table 4.6 shows the finishes/techniques used by the respondents to withstand accidents due to these environmental hazards.

(a) Entire House

Among the selected residents about half (45.50 per cent) of

Table 4.6: Finishes/Techniques used for Selected Factors causing Damage to the Houses (n=200)

S.No.	Area	Factors Causing Damage									
		Termite		Fire		Earthquake		Electric Shock		Dampness	
		F	%	F	%	F	%	F	%	F	%
1	*Entire House*	29	14.50	—	—	—	—	57	28.50	91	45.50
2	*Specific Area*										
	Living Room	63	31.50	—	—	—	—	17	8.50	40	20.00
	Bed Room	40	20.00	—	—	5	2.50	29	14.50	29	14.50
	Kitchen	51	25.50	29	14.50	—	—	23	11.50	40	20.00
	Store Room	40	20.00	—	—	5	2.50	17	8.50	29	14.50
	Bath Room	23	11.50	—	—	—	—	34	17.50	23	11.50
	Stair Cases	5	2.50	—	—	—	—	11	5.50	17	8.50
	Verandah	11	5.50	—	—	5	2.50	—	—	23	11.50

the respondents have given protective finishes to entire house to get rid of problems arising due to dampness especially during rainy season, very few gave treatment for preventing electric shock (28.50 per cent) and termite (14.50 per cent).

(b) Specific Area

It was found that sometimes residents applied finishes or used specific material to withstand accidents. In living room some of the respondents applied finishes against termite (31.50 per cent), dampness (20 per cent) and very few of them for electric shock (8.50 per cent). It was also reported by the respondents that 20 per cent of them used termite resistance for their bedroom and storeroom, 25.50 per cent of them for kitchen and some other areas of the houses. Fire proof materials in kitchen were found only in 14.50 per cent of the houses. Different architectural measures were also used by very few (2.50 per cent) residents to make bed room, store room and verandah earthquake-resistant. Electric shock resistance was provided by the residents usually in bathroom (17 per cent), kitchen (11.50 per cent) and bedroom (14.50 per cent). Various measures were found to be important for damp proofing in living room (20 per cent), bedroom (14.50 per cent), storeroom (14.50 per cent) and kitchen (20 per cent). (Figure 4.7)

It is clear from Table 4.6 that finishes against dampness, electric shock and termite was a common practice among the selected respondents. Some of them also used finishes/techniques to withstand fire, termite and earthquakes. Studies by Turkulin and Sell (2002), Trajkovic *et al.* (1999), Despot *et al.* (1999), Razek (1998) showed the positive effect of finishes on durability of the building materials.

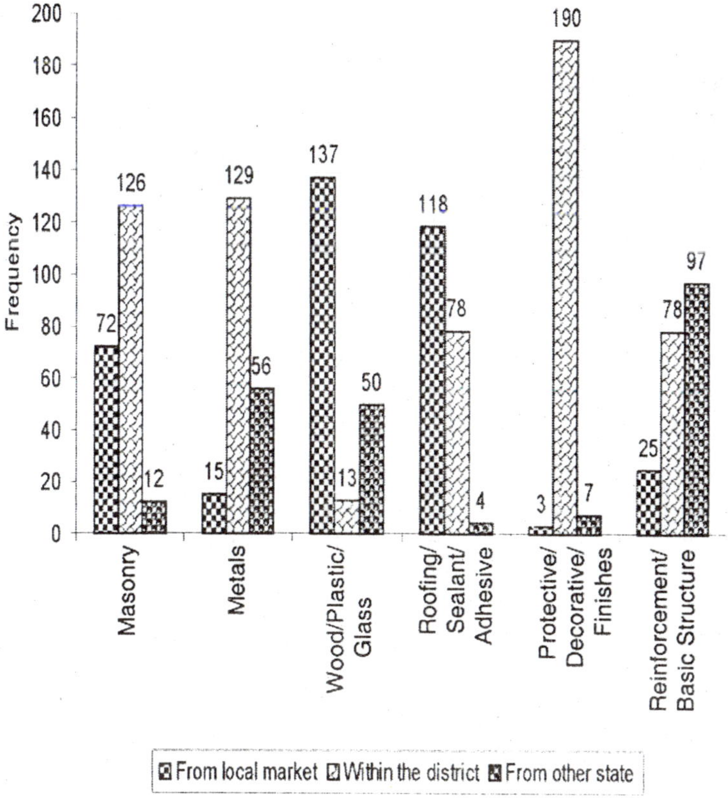

Figure 4.7: Building Materials and their Sources

7. Purpose and Areas Covered by Building Materials Used in Residential Constructions

(a) As Basic Material

Wood was the material used by all the residents (Plates 4.3-4.6) for doors, windows, ventilators, cupboards and half of the respondents for floors, roofs, working counters and staircases whereas, about one-third of them used it for electric fitting boards (33.33 per cent). Stone was also used as basic material (Plates 4.7, 4.8, 4.9) for roofs, cupboards, walls and working counters by about half of the respondents.

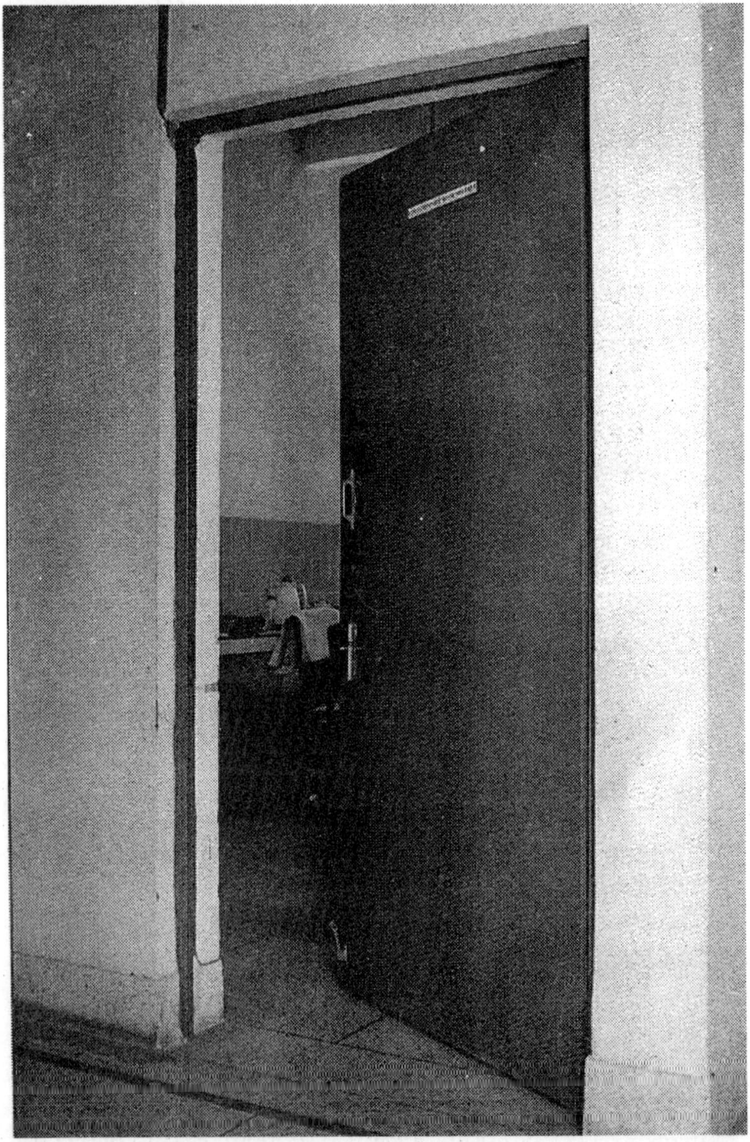

Plate 4.3 : Exterior application of OBM in the House (Source: CBRI, Roorki)

Plate 4.4: Interior application of OBM in the House (Source: CBRI Roorki)

Plate 4.5: Use of Wood in Doors of the House

Plate 4.6: Use of Wood in Roof of the House

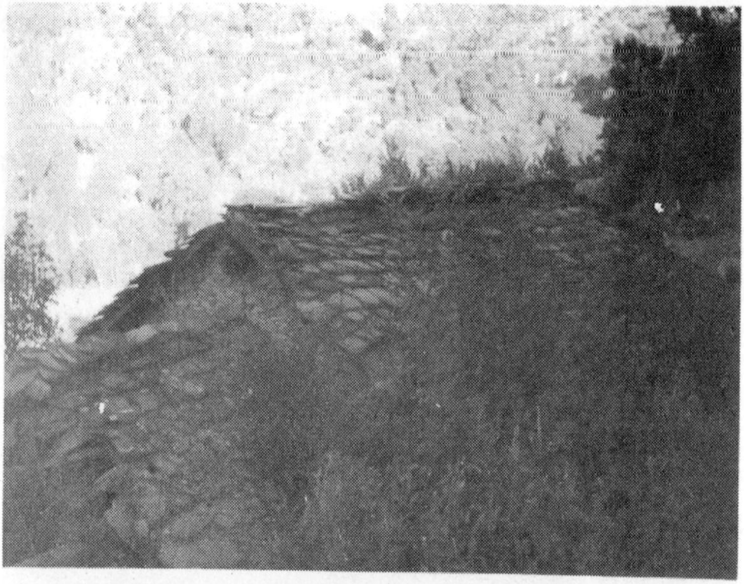

Plate 4.7: Use of Stone in Roof of the House

Plate 4.8: Use of Stone in Stairs of the House

Plate 4.9: Use of Stone in Walls of the House

Agrawal and Jain in their study conducted in 1991, reported that there are various alternative building materials used as substitute for wood such as fibre boards, gypsum boards, PVC boards, EPS sandwich composites, FRP panels etc. Different products, particularly doors and windows are available in Indian market made of these materials and they have been generally used by the people in their homes, despite of, they have not been sufficiently tested for their suitability and performance.

(b) As Finishing Material

Some building materials were used as finishes or supporting material either to add coagulation property or aesthetics to the residences. All the houses used paints on walls, doors, windows, ventilators, cupboards and working counters, windows and ventilators. Plastic was the OBM used by all the respondents for finishing on walls.

Table 4.7 and corresponding plates showed that naturally occurring organic building materials are very much used in the selected area. Some synthetic OBM like polymers were also used to improve functionality, durability and aestheticity in the houses.

8. Extent of Use of Organic Building Materials in the Selected Residential Constructions

The organic building materials used by the respondents in their houses were listed and their extent of use in their houses was determined on the basis of their notations for the use of materials in all the areas, most of the areas and some of the areas. (Table 4.8)

A little less than half of the respondents (44 per cent) reported that they used wood and its products in most of the areas of their residential constructions. Plastics and its derivatives were used by about half of the respondents in most of the areas (55 per cent) and another half of the respondents in some of the areas (45 per cent). Only some of the respondents reported that they used asphalt (12.50 per cent) and bitumen (21.50 per cent) in some of the areas of their home. Resins/adhesives being important building materials were used by all of the respondents in varying degrees, viz. in all of the areas (39.50 per cent), most of the areas (13.50 per cent) and some of the areas (47 per cent) of the home. (Figure 4.8)

Table 4.7: Purpose and Areas Covered by Building Materials Used In Residential Constructions (n=12)

S.No.	Material	Areas Acquired										
		Floors	*Walls*	*Roofs*	*Doors*	*Windows*	*Ventilators*	*Cupboards*	*Working Counters*	*Electric Fittings*	*Plumbing*	*Staircases*
A)	**As Basic Material**											
1	Stone	—	8 66.67	6 50.00	—	—	—	6 50.00	6 50.00	—	—	1 8.33
2.	Bricks	—	4 33.33	—	—	—	—	—	—	—	—	—
3.	Wood	6 50.00	2 16.67	6 50.00	12 100	12 100	12 100	12 100	6 50.00	4 33.33	—	6 50.00
4.	Iron	—	—	—	—	12 100	12 100	—	—	—	—	—
5.	Steel	—	—	—	—	—	—	—	—	—	4 33.33	—
6.	Aluminium	—	—	—	—	—	—	—	—	—	12 100	—
7.	Sand	—	—	—	—	—	—	—	—	—	—	—
8.	Plastic	—	—	—	—	—	—	—	—	8 66.67	—	—

(Contd...)

(Table 4.7 *Contd...*)

(B) As Finishing Material											
1. Stone	5	—	—	—	—	—	—	—	—	—	—
	41.67										
2. Bricks	—	—	—	—	—	—	—	—	—	—	—
3. Wood	—	—	—	—	—	—	—	—	—	—	—
4. Iron	—	—	—	12	12	12	12	—	—	—	—
				100	100	100	100				
5 Steel	—	—	—	—	—	—	—	—	—	—	—
6 Aluminium	—	—	—	—	—	—	—	—	—	—	—
7 Sand	—	—	—	—	—	—	—	—	—	—	—
8 Plastic	—	12	—	—	—	—	—	—	—	—	—
		100									
9 Paint	—	12	6	12	12	12	12	7	—	—	6
		100	50.00	100	100	100	100	58.33			50.00
10 Glass	4	—	—	—	9	10	7	—	—	—	—
	33.33				75.00	83.33	58.33				

Figure in parentheses are percentages of total.

Table 4.8 : Extent of Use of Organic Building Materials in the Selected Residential Constructions (n=200)

S.No.	Organic Building Materials	Extent of Use					
		All the Areas		Most of the Areas		Some of the Areas	
		F	%	F	%	F	%
1.	Wood and its products	35	17.50	88	44.00	77	38.50
2.	Plastics and its derivatives	--	--	110	55.00	90	45.00
3.	Asphalt	--	--	--	--	25	12.50
4.	Bitumen	--	--	--	--	43	21.50
5.	Resins/Adhesives	79	39.50	27	13.50	94	47.00

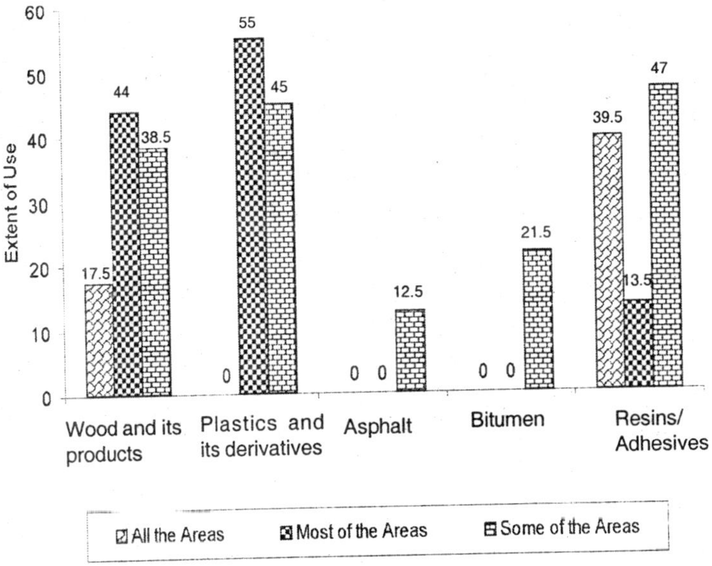

Figure 4.8 : Extent of Use of Organic Building Materials in the Selected Residential Constructions

9. Care and Maintenance in the Residential Constructions

Data in Table 4.9 revealed that most of the respondents took care and maintenance of wash-basins, working counters and bathtub (93.50 per cent), cupboards (89.50 per cent), doors, windows and ventilators (85.50 per cent), roofs and walls (86.50 per cent) on their own. It is clear from the data that most of the care and maintenance was done by the respondents on their own therefore it helped the investigator in finding out the effect of OBM on the health of the respondents, satisfaction of the respondents towards use of OBM and also the problems in the care and maintenance of the house.

The respondents reported that time taken for the care and maintenance of the roofs and walls (83.50 per cent), doors, windows and ventilators (61.50 per cent), wash basins, working counters and bathtub (91 per cent) and stairs and side supports (79 per cent) was 30-60 minutes. Whereas, 60-90 minutes were involved in the care and maintenance of floors (48.50 per cent) and cupboards. But more than 90 minutes were reported for cleaning of cupboards by little less than of the respondents (44 per cent).

It is clear from Table 4.9 that floors were cleaned daily by more than a half of the respondents (69.50 per cent). Care and maintenance of roofs and walls (56.50 per cent), doors, windows and ventilators (72.50 per cent), cupboards (64.50 per cent), washbasins, working counters and bathtub (54.50 per cent) done weekly by more than half of the respondents. Roofs and walls requiring least maintenance was reported by about one third of the respondents (29.50 per cent).

Cost involved in the cleaning and maintenance was reported least (Rs. 0-500 per month) in cupboards by 91 per cent of the respondents and highest (Rs. 1001 and above) in the cleaning of the floors by 11.50 per cent of the respondents. A little less than half of the respondents (43.50 per cent) reported Rs. 501-1000 per month for cleaning and

Table 4.9 : Details of Care and Maintenance in the Residential Constructions (n .= 200)

S. No.	Details	Area of the House											
		Roofs and Walls		Floor		Doors, Windows and Ventilators		Cupboards		Washbasins, working Counters and Bathtub		Stairs and side supports	
		F	%	F	%	F	%	F	%	F	%	F	%
Care and Maintenance													
1.	*Person Involved*												
	Own	173	86.50	121	60.50	171	85.50	179	89.50	187	93.50	93	46.50
	Servant	27	13.50	79	39.50	29	14.50	21	10.50	13	6.50	107	53.50
2.	*Time taken (min.month^{-1})*												
	30-60 minutes	167	83.50	97	48.50	123	61.50	15	7.50	182	91.00	158	79.00
	60-90 minutes	32	16.00	103	51.50	77	38.50	97	48.50	16	8.00	1	0.50
	more than 90 min.	1	0.50	—	—	—	—	88	44.00	2	1.00	41	20.50
3.	*Frequency*												
	Daily	—	—	139	69.50	21	10.50	3	1.50	32	16.00	13	6.50
	Weekly	113	56.50	61	30.50	145	72.50	129	64.50	109	54.50	87	43.50
	Monthly	28	14.00	—	—	27	13.50	62	31.00	59	29.50	48	24.00
	Yearly	59	29.50	11	—	7	3.50	6	3.00	—	—	52	26.00
4.	*Cost Involved*												
	Rs. 0-500	94	47.00	109	54.5	146	73.00	182	91.00	173	86.50	179	89.50
	Rs. 501-1000	87	43.50	68	34.00	43	21.50	7	3.50	27	13.50	18	9.00
	Rs. 1001 and above	19	9.50	23	11.50	11	5.50	11	5.50	—	—	3	1.50

(Contd...)

(Table 4.9 *Contd...*)

5.	*Type of Repair*												
	Own	3	1.50	7	3.50	13	6.50	—	—	—	—	—	—
	Hired	197	98.50	193	96.50	187	93.50	200	100	200	100	200	100
6	*Frequency of Repair*												
	Weekly	—	—	—	—	—	—	—	—	—	—	—	—
	Monthly	—	—	—	—	—	—	—	—	—	—	—	—
	Seasonal	200	100	200	100	200	100	200	100	200	100	200	100
7.	*Cost Involved*												
	Rs. 0-500 (per month)	—	—	19	9.50	39	19.50	—	—	—	—	7	3.50
	Rs. 501-1000 (-do-)	36	18.00	41	20.50	161	80.50	51	25.50	102	51.00	181	90.50
	Rs. 1001 and above	164	82.00	140	70.00	—	—	149	74.50	98	49.00	12	6.00

maintenance of the cupboards. All of the respondents hired people for repair in cupboards, washbasins, working counters and bathtubs and stairs and side supports. But few of the respondents (1.50 per cent) reported that they repaired their roofs and walls on their own. The repair in the areas of the home was seasonal and involved Rs. 1001 and above for roofs (82 per cent), floors (70 per cent), cupboards (74.50 percent). Rs. 501-1000 reported for doors and windows and ventilators (80.50 per cent), stairs and side support (90. 50 per cent).

10. Physical Problems in Various Parts of the Residential Buildings Observed by the Respondents

Glasgow District Council (1989), Hunt, Martin and Platt (1986), Turkulin *et al.* (1997) indicated quite clearly that various external and internal environmental as well as physical factors affects the quality of building materials and they sometimes became causal factors for physical problems in the houses. Several physical problems found generally in houses were asked to the respondents as given in Table 4.10.

Data revealed that in walls major physical problems reported by the respondents were deformity (75 per cent), dampness (77.50 per cent) and flaking off (65 per cent). Fire ignition, termite and reaction with food materials were the problems least reported (2.50 per cent) by the respondents.

Dampness in roofs was found to be a major physical problem in the houses of 62.50 per cent of the respondents and corrosion (2.50 per cent) and noise (5 per cent) were the problems causing least problems for the respondents.

Termite was reported as a major problem in wooden doors (52.50 per cent). Dust release (45 per cent) and corrosion (30 per cent) was also reported by about one- third of the respondents. Vegetative growth and heating up were reported by 2.5 per cent of the respondents only.

More or less same problems as in doors were found in

Table 4.10 : Physical Problems in Various Parts of the Residential Buildings Observed by the Respondents (n=200)

S.No.	Problems	Area of Residential Building											
		Walls		Roof		Doors		Windows		Floor		Cupboard	
		F	%	F	%	F	%	F	%	F	%	F	%
1	Deformity	150	75.00	45	22.50	55	27.50	40	20.00	35	17.50	25	12.50
2	Dampness	155	77.50	125	62.50	30	15.00	15	7.50	15	7.50	30	15.00
3	Flaking off	130	65.00	80	40.00	30	15.00	25	12.50	10	5.00	5	2.50
4	Shorter iife of BM	25	12.50	10	5.00	50	25.00	15	7.50	5	2.50	15	7.50
5	Corrosion	15	7.50	5	2.50	60	30.00	65	32.50	5	2.50	35	17.50
6	Vegetative Growth	55	27.50	25	12.50	5	2.50	10	5.00	10	5.00	5	2.50
7	Fire Ignition	5	2.50	--	--	45	22.50	40	20.00	15	7.50	15	7.50
8	Dust Release	75	37.50	55	27.50	90	45.00	95	47.50	90	45.00	50	25.00
9	Termite	5	2.50	--	--	105	52.50	75	37.50	5	2.50	60	30.00
10	Mold Growth	35	17.50	15	7.50	20	10.00	25	12.50	5	2.50	30	15.00
11	Reaction with Water	20	10.00	20	10.00	45	22.50	15	7.50	15	7.50	10	5.00
12	Reaction with Food Materials	5	2.50	--	--	--	--	--	--	15	7.50	10	5.00
13	Heating up	50	25.00	85	42.50	5	2.50	5	2.50	30	15.00	--	--
14	Noise	20	10.00	10	5.00	45	22.50	50	25.00	15	7.50	10	5.00
15	Fumes	30	15.00	25	12.50	45	22.50	60	30.00	5	2.50	15	7.50
16	Smell	30	15.00	10	5.00	15	7.50	15	7.50	15	7.50	55	27.50

the windows of the houses of the selected respondents. Termite caused deteriorative problems in about a little more than one-third (37.50 per cent) of the houses. Dust release (47.50 per cent) and corrosion (32.50 per cent) was reported by about one-third of the respondents, too. The physical problems in windows least reported by the respondents was heating up.

Floors became problematic due to dust release in about half of the houses (45 per cent). Shorter life of building material, fumes, termite and mold growth were also found as causal factors for deterioration in the houses by some of the respondents (2.50 per cent). In the floors of the selected houses physical problems reported by some of the respondents (2.5 per cent) were shorter life of building material and corrosion.

A little less than one-third of the respondents reported about the termite (30 per cent), dust release (25 per cent) and smell (27.50 per cent) in the cupboards. Whereas, the problems least reported were flaking off and vegetative growth by the 2.50 per cent respondents.

Reasons for the problems reported were excessive water, air, termite in wood, smell due to water; soil, etc., rain, pollution, weeds (*gajar ghas*), garbage, etc.

11. Symptoms of Health Problems Perceived by Respondents in the Residential Constructions

Several studies by Strachan *et al.* (1986); McCarthy *et al.* (1985) and Blackman *et al.* (1989), Boardman (1986) and Smith (1989) have found links among building materials and damp housing, the presence of mould and high rates of asthma and respiratory illness. Various health problems for which building materials found to be a causative factor were asked to the respondents.

Table 4.11a : Rank Order of Symptoms of Health Problems Perceived by Respondents in the Residential Constructions (n = 200)

S. No.	*Symptoms of Health Problems*	*Often*	*Sometimes*	*Never*	*Mean Value*	*Rank Order*
1.	Sneezing	55	100	45	0.683	IX
2.	Dizziness	40	95	65	0.625	XVI
3.	Cough	35	120	45	0.650	XIII
4.	Headache	50	110	40	0.683	X
5.	Nausea	65	75	60	0.576	XX
6.	Fatigue	90	85	25	0.775	II
7.	Excitement	60	100	40	0.370	XXI
8.	Eye Irritation	45	90	65	0.633	XV
9.	Effect on Hearing	90	45	65	0.708	V
10.	Skin Irritation	60	70	70	0.650	XIV
11.	Effect on Visibility	15	130	55	0.600	XVIII
12.	Throat Irritation	55	110	35	0.700	VII
13.	Mental Fatigue	80	35	85	0.658	XI
14.	Chest Tightness	50	60	90	0.600	XIX
15.	Shortness of Breath	70	55	75	0.658	XII
16.	Wheeze	65	35	100	0.608	XVII
17.	Nose Bleeds	75	65	60	0.692	VIII
18.	Dry Skin	70	100	30	0.733	IV
19.	Skin Rash	85	55	60	0.708	VI
20.	Lethargy	90	95	15	0.792	I
21.	Symptoms of Humidifier Fever	80	85	35	0.742	III

Table 4.11a shows that lethargy was the health symptoms due to organic building materials felt by most of the respondents and thus ranked first with a mean value 0.792 among all the perceived health problems. Fatigue was ranked second (0.775) and symptoms of humidifier fever ranked as third (0.742). The health problems perceived least among all were excitement (0.370), nausea (0.576) and chest tightness (0.600).

When the respondents were asked to report on various health problems due to organic building materials used in their houses, most of them (95 per cent) reported that they have a moderate degree of health problems; some of them (4 per cent) perceived the health problems to high extent and only one per cent respondents perceived low extent of the health symptoms. (Table 4.11b and Figure 4.9)

Table 4.11b: Extent of Symptoms of Health Problems Perceived by Respondents in the Residential Constructions (n=200)

S. No.	Extent of Symptoms of Health Problems	Scores	Respondents	
			Frequency	Percentage
1.	High	49-63	8	4.00
2.	Moderate	35-48	190	95.00
3.	Low	21-34	2	1.00

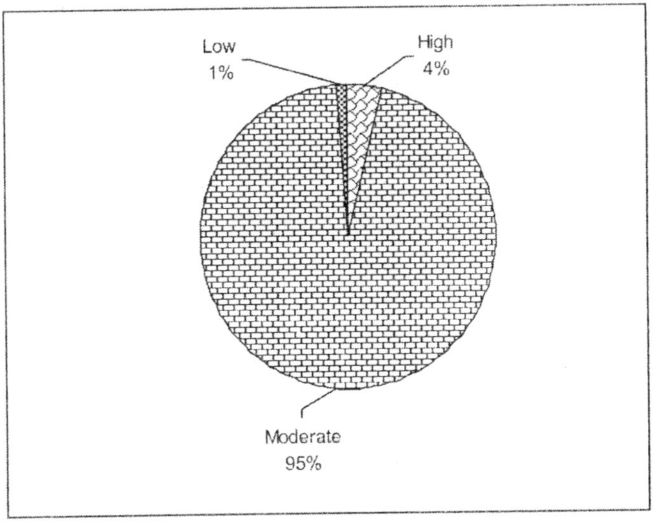

Figure 4.9 : Level of Health Symptoms Perceived by Respondents in the Residential Constructions

12. Health Syndromes Perceived by Respondents in the Residential Constructions

Syndrome is a term used to denote a health problem consisting of various symptoms of ill health. Health syndromes related to buildings were asked to the selected respondents and results are presented in the form of Table 4.12.

Table 4.12 : Health Syndromes reported by Respondents in the Residential Constructions (n=200)

S. No.	Health Syndromes	Major Problem		Minor Problem		No Problem	
		F	%	F	%	F	%
(A)	*Sick Building Syndrome*						
1.	Symptoms of Eye Irritation	—	—	55	27.50	145	72.50
2.	Symptoms of Throat Irritation	5	2.50	50	25.00	145	72.50
3.	Symptoms of nose Irritation	5	2.50	10	5.00	185	92.50
4.	Symptoms of Mucosa of Skin	50	25.00	45	22.50	105	52.50
5.	Mental Fatigue	20	10.00	30	15.00	150	75.00
6.	Arythema	5	2.50	—	—	195	97.50
B	*Building Related Illness*						
1.	Asthma like Symptoms	50	25.00	25	12.50	125	62.50
2.	Legionnaire's Disease	15	7.50	5	2.50	180	90
3.	Hyper Sensitivity	20	10.00	25	12.50	155	77.50
4.	Humidifier Fever	10	5.00	15	7.50	175	87.50
C	*Multiple Chemical Sensitivity*						
1.	Extreme Dust Sensitivity	50	25.00	60	30.00	90	45.00
2.	Chronic Fatigue	20	10.00	45	22.50	135	67.50
3.	Nausea	5	2.50	30	15.00	165	82.50
4.	Headache	20	10.00	50	25.00	130	65.00

It is very much clear from the data given in Table 4.12 that building related health syndromes were found in the respondents residing in the houses of OBM. As far as sick building syndrome was concerned one-fourth of the respondents reported symptoms of throat irritation as minor problem and symptoms of mucosa of skin as major problem. Symptoms of eye irritation were reported as major problem by none of them. Fifteen per cent of the respondents perceived the mental fatigue as a minor health problem.

Among building related illness one-fourth of them reported asthma like symptoms as major problem. Legionnaire's disease was also reported as a major problem by 7.50 per cent of them.

Extreme dust sensitivity was reported as a major problem by 25 per cent of the respondents. About one- fourth of them also reported that they had extreme dust sensitivity (30 per cent), chronic fatigue (22.50 per cent) and headache (25 per cent) as minor problems.

A study conducted by Singh, 1991 also revealed that the prime cause for a large number of fire deaths is the use of new materials, especially organic polymers in buildings both as integral parts and furnishings which are capable of producing wide variety of asphyxiant toxicants. These materials, no doubt have many advantages over inorganic traditional building materials, but some restrictions may be imposed to their use in building to reduce hazardous situations.

13. Level of Knowledge Regarding Organic Building Materials of the Respondents

The most important factor considered in collecting the items for the knowledge test was to include the various aspects of OBM like, their origin, use, constituents, utility, physiological and psychological effect and so on.

The level of knowledge of the respondents is determined in terms of whether they possess good, medium or low knowledge. This is measured by giving scores to answers for each item in the test and by addition of the scores for each respondent.

When respondents were asked several questions regarding OBM they scored 102-135 points and their knowledge level was found as low level by most of them (96.50 per cent). Some of them (3.50 per cent) scored 136-170 points and they fall under category of middle knowledge level regarding OBM. None of them showed high knowledge level. (Figure 4.10)

Thus need was felt to formulate a techno-kit regarding information about knowledge. The package would enhance knowledge of the respondents thus improvement in awareness about OBM used in residential constructions.

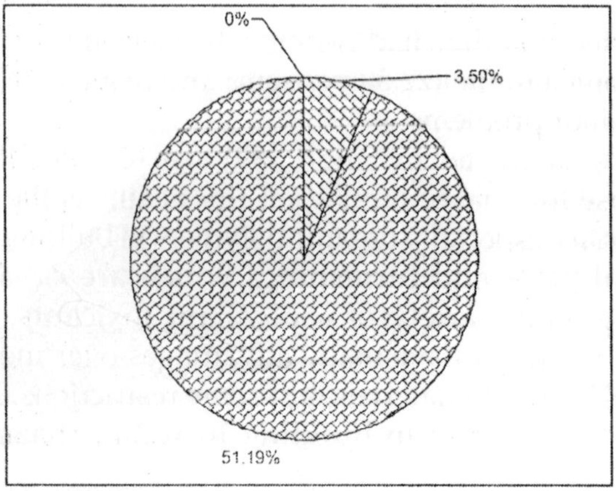

Figure 4.10 : Level of Knowledge Regarding Organic Building Materials of the Respondents

Table 4.12a: Level of Knowledge Regarding Organic Building Materials of the Respondents (n=200)

S.No.	*Level of Knowledge*	*Scores*	*Respondents*	
			F	*%*
1.	Low Level	102-135	193	96.50
2.	Middle Level	136-170	7	3.50
3.	High Level	171-204	0	00.00

14. Satisfaction Derived From Use of OBM in Residential Constructions

Data in Table 4.12b justifies that the satisfaction derived after the use of OBM was ranked on the basis of cost, care and maintenance of house, function/purpose, safety and heath effects. The respondents were highly satisfied by safety and care and maintenance therefore ranked it first for satisfaction level. Function/purpose performed by OBM in home were ranked third. However, no health effects were ranked least.

Among different aspects taken for the satisfaction scale, cost of OBM at initial construction was ranked first and cost

Table 4.12b: Satisfaction Derived from Use of OBM in Residential Constructions (n=200)

S. No.	Item/Statement	Highly Satisfactory		Satisfactory		Not Satisfactory		Mean Values	Rank Order (A)	Rank Order (B)
		F	%	F	%	F	%			
(A)	COST									
1	Cost of OBM at initial construction	64	32.00	55	27.50	81	40.50	0.64	III	
2	Cost of OBM at time of renovation/repair	85	42.50	79	39.50	36	18.00	0.75	I	
3	Cost involved in cleaning	76	38.00	43	21.50	81	40.50	0.66	II	II
4	Cost involved in heating of home	43	21.50	42	21.00	39	19.50	0.42	VI	
5	Cost involved in cooling of home	49	24.50	118	59.00	33	16.50	0.56	V	
6	Cost involved in transportation of products	37	18.50	97	48.50	66	33.00	0.62	IV	
(B)	CARE AND MAINTENANCE									
1	Number of persons needed to be involved while cleaning	46	23.00	100	50.00	54	27.00	0.65	III	
2	Frequency of care to be done	79	39.50	37	18.50	84	42.00	0.66	II	I
3	Time involved in cleaning	61	30.50	79	39.50	60	30.00	0.67	I	
4	Time involved in repair	49	24.50	73	36.50	78	39.00	0.62	IV	

(Table 4.12b *Contd...*)

(C) FUNCTION/PURPOSE									
1	Heating in winters	34	17.00	94	47.00	72	36.00	0.60	VII	
2	Cooling in summers	43	21.50	64	32.00	93	46.50	0.59	VIII	
3	Noise control	82	41.00	76	38.00	42	21.00	0.73	I	
4	Durability	73	36.50	72	36.00	55	27.50	0.70	II	
5	Strength	55	27.50	73	36.50	72	36.00	0.64	V	III
6	Damp proofing	49	24.50	88	44.00	63	31.50	0.65	IV	
7	Light in weight	82	41.00	58	29.00	60	30.00	0.70	II	
8	Aestheticity	52	26.00	73	36.50	75	37.50	0.63	VI	
9	Fire proofing	67	33.50	58	29.00	73	36.50	0.65	IV	
10	Dust control	72	36.00	67	33.50	61	30.50	0.69	III	
(D) SAFETY										
1	Electric shock proof	58	29.00	69	34.50	39	19.50	0.59	III	
2	Damp proof	78	39.00	97	48.50	25	12.50	0.76	I	
3	Earthquake resistant	25	12.50	78	39.00	97	48.50	0.55	IV	
4	Fire proof	34	17.00	85	42.50	81	40.50	0.59	III	I
5	Termite proof	82	41.00	81	40.50	49	24.50	0.76	I	
6	Allergy level	31	15.50	133	66.50	36	18.00	0.66	II	
7	Chemical reactions	25	12.50	145	72.50	30	15.00	0.66	II	
(E) HEALTH EFFECTS: Respondents experienced no effect regarding:										
1	Skin allergies	25	12.50	148	74	27	13.50	0.67	I	
2	Bad odors	19	9.50	129	64.50	52	26.00	0.61	V	
3	Eye irritation	28	14.00	127	63.50	45	22.50	0.64	III	
4	Respiratory problems	16	8.00	139	69.50	45	22.50	0.62	IV	

(Contd...)

(**Table 4.12b** *Contd...*)

5	Fatigue or activeness	13	6.50	144	72.00	43	21.50	0.62	IV	IV
6	Throat infection	10	5.00	129	64.50	61	30.50	0.58	VII	
7	Headache	16	8.00	138	69.00	46	23.00	0.62	IV	
8	Hypersensitivity	19	9.50	121	60.50	60	30.00	0.60	VI	
9	Chemical reactions	58	29.00	81	40.50	61	30.50	0.66	II	

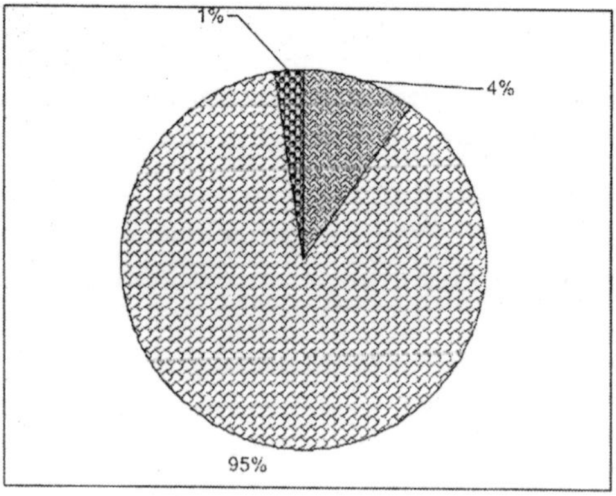

Figure 4.11: Extent of Satisfaction Derived from Use of OBM in Residential Construction

Table 4.13: Extent of Satisfaction Derived from Use of OBM in Residential Constructions (n=200)

S.No.	*Satisfaction Level*	*Scores*	*Respondents*	
			F	%
1.	Low Level	36-60	8	4.00
2.	Middle Level	61-84	191	95.50
3.	High Level	85-108	1	00.50

involved in cooling and heating were ranked lasts for aspects of costs involved in OBM constructions. For care and maintenance, the respondents were satisfied utmost with time involved in cleaning and the least satisfied with the time involved in repair. It inferred that if there was any defect in the building areas of OBM then it involved lot of money and efforts to be wasted. For functional purposes of OBM noise and light was efficiently controlled thus the respondents were satisfied with the purposes of OBM. Cooling in summers was the purpose with which the respondents were least satisfied. Among safety aspects, termite proof and damp proof were the aspects the respondents were highly satisfied.

For cost of OBM about half of the respondents (42.50 per cent) were satisfied by its cost at the time of repair/ renovation. As no health effects were ranked least on the satisfaction level, about more than half of the respondents were not satisfied with no skin allergies (67 per cent), no chemical reactions (66 per cent), no eye irritation (64 per cent), no respiratory problems (62 per cent) and no fatigue or activeness (62 per cent).

The results for some of the aspects reported by the respondents did not match with the problems reported earlier. The reason might be that in due course of time they got used to the problems.

Extent of satisfaction in Table 4.13 showed that most of the respondents showed middle level of satisfaction (95.50 per cent) scoring 61- 84 points on the satisfaction scale. However, some of the respondents showed low level of satisfaction (4 per cent) by scoring 36-60 points. But only 00.50 per cent of the respondents showed high level of satisfaction after using OBM in the home.

SECTION: 4.3
EXPERIMENTAL RESULTS

Experiments for the study were carried out on a sample of twelve respondents in the selected area. In order to find out the defects in the house and performance of the respondents living in the wooden and non-wooden houses as these were the two commonly used basic materials for residential constructions. Therefore a set of six wooden and six non-wooden houses was selected and the observations were recorded. Care was taken to select houses with similar age, size and orientation.

The section deals with checklist of defective symptoms/ problems in the residential constructions, parameters of human performance and environment in houses constructed with OBM.

15. Checklist of Defective Symptoms/Problems in the Residential Constructions (Bowyer, 1973)

Checklist of defective symptoms in various parts of building structures given by Bowyer, 1973 was used to observe physical problems in the selected residential constructions. Observations showed that in wooden homes, roofs were showing dampness (50 per cent), rot (33.33 per cent), stains (33.33 per cent) and splits (33.33 per cent). Cracks (50 per cent), dirty spots (33.33 per cent), fractured areas (33.33 per cent) and dampness (33.33 per cent) were observed in the walls. Rot (33.33 per cent) and stains (33.33 per cent) were quite observable in floors and staircases (timber) of the selected wooden houses. Deposition of dirt was observed in all of the wooden houses. When internal finishes were observed it was found that in half of the houses cracks were found and about one-third (33.33 per cent) of the houses were showing loss of gloss and misses in the painting. Problems like leakage (33.33 per cent), smell of heating (16.67 per cent), lack of temperature (16.67 per cent), spots (16.67 per cent) and fungus (50 per cent) were also observed in the wooden houses.

Observations in non-wooden houses showed that in roofs the major problem was infestation in about more than three-fourth (83.33 per cent) of the houses. Whereas, granular surface in half of the houses (50 per cent), dampness in a little more than a half (66.67 per cent) was observed. When walls were observed dirty spots and dampness were observed in all of the houses. Dirt (100 per cent) and stains (66.67 per cent) were the defective symptoms observed – in floors and staircases. Internal finishes were showing cracks in half of the houses and loss of gloss and flaking were problems found in 66.67 per cent of the houses. Services were also hindered due to leakage (66.67 per cent) and lack of temperature (50 per cent).

Inference drawn from the above data is that in case of roofs, wooden houses were showing more defective

Table 4.14 : Checklist of Defective Symptoms/Problems in the Residential Constructions (n = 12)

S. No.	*Defective Symptoms/Problems*	*Residential Constructions*			
		Wooden (n=6)		*Non-Wooden (n=6)*	
		F	*%*	*F*	*%*
(A) ROOF					
1.	Rot	2	33.33	1	16.67
2.	Splits	2	33.33	—	—
3.	Granular surface	—	—	3	50.00
4.	Crumbled on surface	1	16.67	—	—
5.	Loosen paving	1	16.67	—	—
6.	Dampness	3	50.00	4	66.67
7.	No grating	—	—	—	—
8.	Bubbles on surface	—	—	—	—
9.	Dirt	6	100	—	—
10.	Stains	2	33.33	1	16.67
11.	Infestation	1	16.67	5	83.33
(B) WALLS					
1.	Cracks	3	50.00	1	16.67
2.	Rot	—	—	—	—
3.	Twisted /Curled	—	—	—	—
4.	Dirty Spots	2	33.33	6	100
5.	Fractured	2	33.33	—	—
6.	Dampness	2	33.33	6	100
7.	Dry dirty patch	—	—	—	—
8.	Sagging timber lining	—	—	—	—
9.	Damp rising on internal walls	—	—	—	—
(C) FLOORS AND STAIRCASES (TIMBER)					
1.	Rot	2	33.33	—	—
2.	Board crack underfoot	1	16.67	—	—
3.	White spongy under floor covering	—	—	—	—
4.	Bay dips outward	1	16.67	—	—
5.	Stains	2	33.33	4	66.67
6.	Long filament growth	1	16.67	—	—
7.	1st floor unstable under foot cracks	1	16.67	—	—
8.	Olive green or brown fruiting body on surfaces	—	—	—	—
9.	Squeaks the staircases	—	—	—	—
10.	Tread fall away	—	—	—	—
11.	Small holes	1	16.67	—	—
12.	Dirt	6	100	6	100
13.	Saw dust	1	16.67	—	—

(Contd...)

(Table 4.14 Contd...)

(D) INTERNAL FINISHES				
I. PLASTER				
1. Crack	3	50.00	3	50.00
2. Soft and crumbly	—	—	—	—
3. Dry and crumbly	—	—	—	—
4. Dampness	1	16.67	—	—
5. Bulging	—	—	—	—
6. Pinholes in joinery	—	—	—	—
7. Blister or small crater	—	—	—	—
II PAINTING				
1. Bittiness	—	—	—	—
2. Blooming	—	—	—	—
3. Cissing	—	—	—	—
4. Drying trouble	—	—	—	—
5. Grinning	—	—	—	—
6. Mould	—	—	—	—
7. Shriveling	—	—	—	—
8. Bleeding	—	—	—	—
9. Brush marks	1	16.67	1	16.67
10. Crazing	—	—	—	—
11. Efflorescence	—	—	—	—
12. Loss of gloss	2	33.33	4	66.67
13. Poor opacity	1	16.67	—	—
14. Saponification	—	—	—	—
15. Blistering	—	—	—	—
16. Chalking	—	—	—	—
17. Running	—	—	—	—
18. Flaking	2	33.33	4	66.67
19. Misses	—	—	—	—
20. Sheeriness	—	—	—	—
(E) SERVICES				
1. Leakage	2	33.33	4	66.67
2. Noisy	—	—	—	—
3. Encrustation	—	—	—	—
4. Fungus	3	50.00	1	16.67
5. Water stain	—	—	1	16.67
6. Supply sluggish	—	—	—	—
7. Lack of temperature	1	16.67	3	50.00
8. Excessive joints	—	—	—	—
9 Spots	1	16.67	—	—
10 Smell of heating	1	16.67	1	16.67

symptoms than the non-wooden houses. In walls of non-wooden houses, the problems of dirty spots and dampness were prominent. Floors and staircases of timber were more exposed to rot, cracking (Plates 4.12 and 4.13), stains, long filament growth and small holes. In wooden houses as well as non-wooden houses, internal finishes were defective with

Plate 4.12: Cracking in Balcony made up of Wood

Plate 4.13: Cracking in Floor made up of Wood

cracks, dampness (Plate 4.14), brush marks, loss of gloss and poor opacity. In case of service like water supply, electricity, etc. defective symptoms were more or less same in case of both the types of houses.

Plate 4.14 : Cracking and Flaking off due to Dampness in Building

16. Parameters of Human Performance (short-term memory, attention/concentration, work and fatigue in semi-simplicit activity)

Berglund *et al.* in 1987 designed to study sick building syndrome with a battery of diverse psychological tests (reaction time, short-term memory, vigilance, and steadiness) to assess human performance. The trends were found in the expected direction. Memory is considered central to all cognitive functions and it was tested with a commonly used short-term memory task (Peterson *et al.* 1959).

(a) Short-Term Memory of the Residents

It is a common experience that numbers are difficult to

remember. It has been shown (Peterson & Peterson, 1959) that short-term memory decays rapidly. A standardized test to test short-term memory given by Ost, 1969 (Annexure-3) and further used by many experimentalists was used to test short-term memory of the respondents living in two different types of houses.

Table 4.15 depicts the results of experiment carried out on twelve respondents, six each in wooden and non-wooden houses. The experimenter read a number, then a category name for example, fruits, colours, cities or animals. The subject gave three examples of the category, and then was asked to repeat the same number. The answer was scored as correct or wrong. The digits were read evenly, one each second, then the category name is given in rhythm. The subjects were asked to give examples of the category immediately, with no pause to rehearse the number. Number of mistakes done by each of the respondent in one digit number to seven digit number category was recorded to find out the short-term memory of the respondents.

Table 4.15 : Short-Term Memory of the Residents (n=12)

*Treatment**	*Subject*	*Number of Mistakes Done (0-4 mistakes)*						
		One digit	*Two digits*	*Three digits*	*Four digits*	*Five digits*	*Six digits*	*Seven digits*
T_1	S_1	—	—	—	1	—	3	2
	S_2	—	—	—	3	1	—	4
	S_3	—	2	—	2	—	—	3
	S_4	—	—	1	—	1	3	3
	S_5	—	—	—	1	—	2	3
	S_6	—	—	—	2	1	—	3
T_2	S_1	—	1	—	—	—	2	1
	S_2	—	-	1	—	—	2	2
	S_3	—	—	—	1	—	—	2
	S_4	—	1	—	—	—	—	3
	S_5	—	—	—	—	1	2	2
	S_6	—	—	1	—	—	3	3

* T_1: Wooden Houses T_2: Non-Wooden Houses

Figure 4.12 shows that numbers of niistakes done by the respondents living in houses completely build up of natural OBM i.e. wood was lower than the respondents living in non-wooden houses.

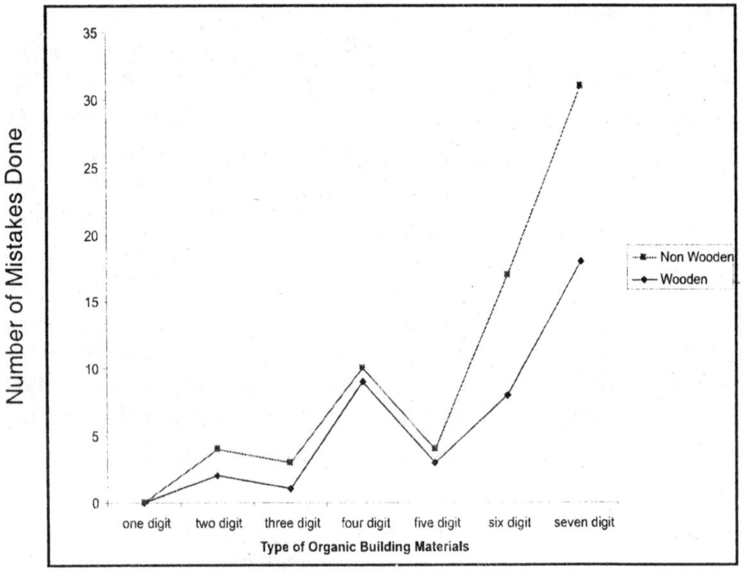

Figure 4.12 : Number of Mistakes Done by the Respondents showing Short-term Memory (n=12)

(b) Attention/Concentration of the Residents

To discover number of times attention wanders and to find out conditions which help concentration or attention, a standardized test for testing attention/concentration given by Kuppuswamy (1954) was used (Annexure-3).

Instructions were given to respondents: 'Look at your pencil. Concentrate your attention upon it for one minute when your attention wanders from the object indicate by a movement of your left hand.' Experimenter noted down the number of times attention wandered during the one minute period.

In the second series the following instructions were given. 'Look at the pencil. Think about its size, colour, material, with which it is made, flaws in the making, its uses, etc. Indicate as before when attention wanders.' Experimenter noted down the number of times attention wandered during the one minute period. The number of time attention wandered in the first series and in the second series were calculated. The difference was noted. The data for whole sample were collected. Mean and S.D. for the two series were calculated. (Table 4.16)

Table 4.16 : Attention/Concentration of the Residents (n=12)

*Treatment**	*Subject*	*Number of times attention wanders*	
		Series 1	*Series 2*
T_1	S_1	2	3
	S_2	2	2
	S_3	3	1
	S_4	0	0
	S_5	0	1
	S_6	1	0
T_2	S_1	1	0
	S_2	0	0
	S_3	1	0
	S_4	4	0
	S_5	0	0
	S_6	0	1
Mean		1.167	0.667
S.D.		±1.348	±0.985

* T_1: Wooden Houses T_2: Non-Wooden Houses

Figure 4.13 shows level of concentration/attention shown by the people living in houses made up of two different types of building materials. It is clear from the Figure 4.13 that poor concentration level was shown by the respondents living in non-wooden houses.

Figure 4.13 : Attention/Concentration of the Residents

(c) Work and Fatigue in Semi-Simplicit Activity

To measure continuous thinking work and its change, especially changes by fatigue, a standardized test for testing work and fatigue in semi-simplicit activity was used (Dashiell, 1931; Watson; Robinson; Pillsbury; Gates).

Subject (S) was comfortably seated in a quiet room. Experimenter (E) pronounced aloud a number. S was immediately asked to add 2 to this number aloud, then asked to add 3 to this new number aloud, then 4 to that, then 5 and then again 2, 3, 4, 5, etc., in rotation. For instance, if the number given was 9, the consecutive sums would be: 11, 14, 18, 23, 28, 32, 37, 39, etc. Every thirty seconds E was to announce a new number with which S was to start at once a new number keep adding throughout at your maximum speed.

Taking first some column of numbers, E offered S a trial by speaking aloud the number at the top, and checked her accuracy in the adding by following down the column. If a mistake was made the correct number was called out and at the same time made a dot opposite it on the page.

For the formal experiments, E used the columns in their order from left to right. The numbers announced every thirty seconds to S were the ones at the top of the columns. As S added aloud, E followed down each column and corrected and marked errors. At the end of each thirty seconds he drawn a line under the last number given by S to indicate how many numbers were added and at the same time announces aloud the new number of the next column.

One person as S was to work constantly in one single bodily position until he had been taken over twenty columns three times — a total of 30 minutes of adding time. She seated looking at a point on the wall and throughout his work she did not vary her bodily posture, but kept the same sitting position, both feet flat on the floor, head and arms in the same pose, etc. This was important. The number of sums done and the mistakes were recorded for each of the respondents as given in Table 4.17.

Table 4.17: Work and Fatigue in Semi-Simplicit Activity (n=12)

*Treatment**	*Subject*	*Number of Sums Done*	*Number of Mistakes Occurred (30 sets)*
T_1	S_1	271	12
	S_2	253	10
	S_3	213	9
	S_4	109	5
	S_5	268	11
	S_6	213	7
T_2	S_1	277	18
	S_2	252	16
	S_3	217	14
	S_4	128	8
	S_5	262	17
	S_6	217	14

* T_1: Wooden Houses T_2: Non-Wooden Houses

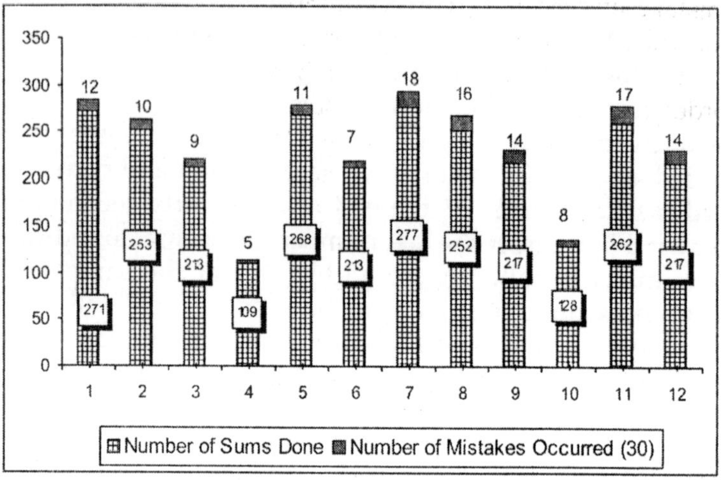

Figure 4.14 : Work and fatigue in Semi-Simplicit Activity

Figure 4.14 revealed that number of sums done by the respondents living in the non-wooden houses were more than the sums done by the respondents living in wooden houses. But, number of mistakes performed by the respondents was more by the respondents living in the wooden houses were more than the sums done by the respondents living in non-wooden houses. It shows that level of fatigue was reflected more by the respondents living in non-wooden houses.

17. Parameters of Indoor Environment

Azer, *et al.* (1972) provides more evidence that hot conditions have significant affects on performance only when they cause a rise in body temperature. Relative humidity seemed to be a key determinant of performance in a variety of tasks. Studies conducted by Allen and Fischer (1978), Barros (1993), I. I. D. A. (1993) also supported the same view point that temperature and humidity are the key determinants of the human performance of the people living in residential unit. Symptoms of poor health also reported if the environmental conditions persist for a longer time.

Data in Table 4.18 shows temperature and humidity values recorded with standardized Thermohygro clock during morning, noon, evening and mid-night simultaneously in wooden and non-wooden houses. The data were further analyzed to find out the difference in the parametric values, thus to estimate evidences of effect of building materials on indoor environment in the selected houses.

There were two types of treatment and six subjects under each treatment. Three sets of temperature values and humidity values were recorded at the same point of time in each of the set of houses. Then values were summed up and average values were quoted so that error could be eliminated. The process was repeated in each set of the houses for morning, noon, evening and mid-night. It was checked that any variation in the data is not due to the cooling or heating devices, prospect of the houses and error in noting down the readings. From the data a clear difference was found in the temperature and humidity in the selected group of houses.

Table 4.18 : Temperature and Humidity of the Selected Residences (n=12)

*Treatment**	*Subject*	*Temperature*					*Humidity*				
		Outdoors	*Indoors*				*Outdoors*	*Indoors*			
		^0C	*M*	*N*	*E*	*MN*	*%*	*M*	*N*	*E*	*MN*
T_1	S_1	13-22	15.3	14.8	15.4	17.1	53	49	41	47	49
	S_2	12-22	15.4	15.5	15.3	15.4	25	49	42	47	48
	S_3	12-22	15.4	16.5	15.3	15.3	24	46	43	49	49
	S_4	12-22	14.8	16.9	16.2	15.5	25	42	38	37	41
	S_5	12-22	14.6	17.2	15.9	15.8	24	43	37	37	40
	S_6	12-23	14.6	15.9	15.7	15.7	23	43	37	40	43
Mean			15.0	16.1	15.6	15.8		45	40	43	45
T_2	S_1	13-22	20.0	20.1	20.0	20.0	53	43	33	41	45
	S_2	12-22	20.0	20.1	20.0	20.0	25	43	33	43	50
	S_3	12-22	20.0	20.1	20.0	20.0	24	43	33	45	51
	S_4	12-22	20.0	20.0	20.0	20.0	25	50	44	34	41
	S_5	12-22	20.0	20.0	20.0	20.0	24	50	45	35	41
	S_6	12-23	20.0	20.0	20.0	20.0	23	50	42	40	43
	Mean			20.0	20.1	20	20	47	38	40	45

* T_1: Wooden Houses T_2: Non-Wooden Houses

In Table 4.18 a clear difference was found in the temperature and humidity in the selected group of houses. The percentage increase in temperature from outdoor to indoor environment was more in non-wooden houses than the wooden houses. But the results were *viceversa* for the relative humidity.

SECTION: 4.4

TESTING OF HYPOTHESIS

A number of hypotheses were formulated on the basis of objectives of the study. For the purpose of statistical analysis the hypotheses were formulated in null form.

To test the hypotheses statistically Analysis of Variance, Pearson's Product Moment Coefficient of Correlation,'t' test and regression analysis were applied.

Analysis of variance was computed to find out the variation due to personal variables, family variables and situational variables towards knowledge regarding OBM, extent of use of OBM in home, problems faced in care and maintenance of the house, satisfaction derived from use of OBM and effect on health of the residents.

To find the variation between the different groups of respondents according to environmental and psycho-logical parameters of performance of the residents 't' test was performed.

Pearson's Product Moment Coefficient of Correlation was computed in order to find degree of relationship among knowledge regarding OBM, extent of use of OBM in home and problems faced in its care and maintenance. Their association with satisfaction derived from use of OBM and effect on health of the residents was also computed.

$H_{0\text{-}1}$: Knowledge regarding OBM, extent of use of OBM in home and problems faced in care and maintenance do not vary with personal variables, family variables and situational variables.

- *Personal Variables*
  - Age
  - Educational qualification
  - Employment status
- *Family Variables*
  - Family size
  - Occupational status
  - Family income
- *Situational Variables*
  - Location of the house
  - Occupancy period
  - Age of building structure

Analysis of variance was computed to test this hypothesis.

(a) Knowledge regarding OBM of the Selected Respondents

Analysis of variance was computed and results showed that, the knowledge regarding OBM of the respondents varied significantly with age (F=2.70), educational qualification (F=4.75), employment status (F=5.75), occupational status (F=5.04) and location of house (F=5.09), which indicated that the knowledge varied due to these variables. Family income, family size, occupancy period and age of building structure which were have no significant impact on knowledge of the respondents. (Table 4.19)

Thus the hypothesis was rejected for the association of the knowledge regarding OBM of the respondents with age, educational qualification, employment status, occupational status and location of house and accepted for family income, family size, occupancy period and age of building structure.

Table 4.19 : Analysis of Variance for Knowledge regarding OBM of the Selected Respondents

Source of Variation	Degree of Freedom	Sum of Squares	Mean of Squares	F Value	Significance Level
Personal Variables					
Age	3.00	893.46	297.82	2.70	0.05
	196.00	21300.00	108.67		
Educational	2.00	1169.63	584.81	4.74	0.01
Qualification	197.00	24300.41	123.35		
Employment	1.00	3134.14	3134.14	5.75	0.01
Status	198.00	107833.68	544.61		
Family Variables					
Family Size	2.00	28.00	14.00	0.74	N.S.
	197.00	373.00	18.90		
Occupational	2.00	2631.30	1315.65	5.04	0.01
Status	197.00	51391.52	1315.65		
Family Income	2.00	667.19	333.59	0.43	N.S.
	197.00	197.00	151528.63		
Situational Variables					
Location of House	1.00	67.28	67.28	5.09	0.05
	198.00	2616.54	13.21		
Age of Building	1.00	45.98	45.98	1.37	N.S.
Structure	198.00	6637.84	33.52		
Occupancy Period	1.00	14.78	14.78	0.44	N.S.
	198.00	6669.04	33.68		

(b) Extent of use of OBM in the Homes of the Selected Respondents

Further, analysis of variance for extent of use of OBM in home was computed and it was found that it varied significantly with educational qualification (F= 6.33), occupational status (F= 17.00), family size (F= 10.12), family income (F= 4.67), location of house (F= 5.91) and age of building structure (F= 10.00). Extent of use of OBM was not found significantly associated with age of the respondent, employment status and occupancy period. (Table 4.20)

Table 4.20 : Analysis of Variance for Extent of Use of OBM in the Homes of the Selected Respondents

Source of Variation	*Degree of Freedom*	*Sum of Squares*	*Mean of Squares*	*F Value*	*Significance Level*
Personal Variables					
Age	3.00	8.40	2.80	0.16	N.S.
	196.00	3472.62	17.72		
Educational	2.00	0.38	0.19	6.33	0.01
Qualification	197.00	6.33	0.03		
Employment Status	1.00	0.40	0.40	0.45	N.S.
	198.00	176.32	0.89		
Family Variables					
Family Size	2.00	0.33	0.165	10.12	0.01
	197.00	3.21	0.0163		
Occupational Status	2.00	1.02	0.51	17.00	0.01
	197.00	5.70	0.03		
Family Income	2.00	0.29	0.14	4.67	0.01
	197.00	06.43	0.03		
Situational Variables					
Location of House	1.00	5.12	5.12	5.91	0.05
	198.00	171.60	0.87		
Age of Building	1.00	10.00	10.00	10.00	0.01
Structure	198.00	0.72	0.00		
Occupancy Period	1.00	0.41	0.41	0.42	N.S.
	198.00	196.98	0.99		

Therefore, the hypothesis was rejected for extent of use of OBM in home with educational qualification, occupational status, family size, family income, location of house and age of building structure and accepted with age of the respondent, employment status and occupancy period.

(c) Problems Faced in Care and Maintenance of the Home by the Selected Respondents

Analysis of variance was applied for problems faced in care and maintenance of the home and the values of the F test showed a significant variation with age (F = 4.83), educational qualification (F = 4.75), employment status (F = 23.34), family size (F = 19.26), location of the house (F = 32.89)

and occupancy period (F = 234.50). Non-significant variation was found with the variable; occupational status, family income and age of building structure.

The hypothesis was rejected for problems faced in care and maintenance of the home with age, educational qualification, employment status, family size, location of the house and occupancy period. It was accepted for occupational status, family income and age of building structure.

Table 4.21 : Analysis of Variance for Problems Faced in Care and Maintenance of the Home by the Selected Respondents

Source of Variation	*Degree of Freedom*	*Sum of Squares*	*Mean of Squares*	*F Value*	*Significance Level*
Personal Variables					
Age	3.00	41.67	13.89	4.83	0.05
	8.00	23.00	2.875		
Educational Qualification	2.00	32.67	16.33	4.75	0.05
	9.00	31.00	3.44		
Employment Status	1.00	22.17	22.17	23.34	0.01
	10.00	9.50	0.95		
Family Variables					
Family Size	2.00	1.04	0.52	19.26	0.01
	9.00	5.30	0.027		
Occupational Status	1.00	22.87	22.87	2.10	N.S.
	10.00	108.80	10.88		
Family Income	2.00	35.33	17.67	1.65	N.S.
	9.00	96.33	10.70		
Situational Variables					
Location of House	1.00	147.00	147.00	32.89	0.01
	10.00	44.67	4.47		
Age of Building Structure	1.00	0.11	0.11	1.83	N.S.
	10.00	0.56	0.06		
Occupancy Period	1.00	4.69	4.69	234.50	0.01
	10.00	0.22	0.02		

$H_{0\text{-}2}$: **There is no inter-relationship among knowledge regarding OBM, extent of use of OBM in home and problems faced in its care and maintenance.**

Pearson's Product Moment of correlation coefficient was calculated to test this hypothesis. Significant relationship was observed between extent of use of OBM in home and problems faced in its care and maintenance; knowledge regarding OBM and problems faced in its care and maintenance. Whereas, relationship of knowledge regarding OBM and extent of use of OBM in home was found non-significant. (Table 4.22)

Table 4.22 : Correlation Coefficient Showing Relationship among Knowledge Regarding OBM, Extent of Use of OBM in Home and Problems Faced in its Care and Maintenance by the Selected Respondents

Variables	*r-values*	*Degree of Freedom*	*Significance Level*
Knowledge regarding OBM and extent of use of OBM in home	0.054729	199	N.S.
Extent of use of OBM in home and problems faced in its care and maintenance	0.99764	199	0.01
Knowledge regarding OBM and problems faced in its care and maintenance	0.72698	199	0.01

$H_{0\text{-}3}$: Knowledge regarding OBM, extent of use of OBM in home and problems faced in care and maintenance of the houses do not vary with satisfaction derived from use of OBM and effect on health of the residents.

Thus, hypothesis was rejected for extent of use of OBM in home and problems faced in its care and maintenance; knowledge regarding OBM and problems faced in its care and maintenance and accepted for relationship of knowledge regarding OBM and extent of use of OBM in home.

To test this hypothesis Pearson's Product Moment of correlation coefficient was computed. The relationship was found significant for extent of use of OBM in home and effect on health, problems faced in care and maintenance of the houses and satisfaction derived from use of OBM and problems faced in care and maintenance of the houses and effect on health. Non significant values were observed for association among knowledge regarding OBM and satisfaction derived from use of OBM, knowledge regarding OBM and effect on health and extent of use of OBM in home and satisfaction derived from use ofOBM.

Table 4.23 : Correlation Coefficient Showing Relationship among Knowledge Regarding OBM, Extent of Use of OBM in Home and Problems faced in its Care and Maintenance by the Selected Respondents

Variables	*r-values*	*Degree of Freedom*	*Significance Level*
Knowledge regarding OBM and satisfaction derived from use of OBM	0.03477	199	N.S.
Knowledge regarding OBM and effect on health	0.00952	199	N.S.
Extent of use of OBM in home and satisfaction derived from use of OBM	0.032274	199	N.S.
Extent of use of OBM in home and effect on health	0.848201	199	0.01
Problems faced in care and maintenance of the houses and satisfaction derived from use of OBM	0.968512	199	0.01
Problems faced in care and maintenance of the houses and effect on health	0.888242	199	0.01

Therefore, hypothesis was rejected for extent of use of OBM in home and effect on health, problems faced in care and maintenance of the houses and satisfaction derived from use of OBM and problems faced in care and maintenance of the houses and effect on health and it was accepted for knowledge regarding OBM and satisfaction derived from use of OBM, knowledge regarding OBM and effect on health and extent of use of OBM in home and satisfaction derived from use of OBM.

Satisfaction derived from use of OBM and effect on health of the residents does not vary with personal variables, family variables and situational variables.

- *Personal Variables*
  - Age
  - Educational qualification
  - Employment status
- *Family Variables*
  - Family size
  - Occupational status
  - Family income
- *Situational Variables*
  - Location of the house
  - Occupancy period
  - Age of building structure

(a) Satisfaction Derived from Use of OBM in the Home by the Selected Respondents

On analysis of variance it was observed that satisfaction derived from use of OBM in the home, it varied significantly with age (F = 42.83), family size (F = 49.09), family income (F = 9.68), location of the house (F = 14.41), occupancy period (F = 9.38) and age of the building structure (F = 31.52). It was found that satisfaction derived not varied significantly with educational qualification, employment status and occupation of the family.

Therefore, hypothesis was rejected for age, family size, family income, location of the house, occupancy period and age of the building structure and accepted for educational qualification, employment status and occupation of the family.

(b) Effect on Health of the Residents by the Selected Respondents

Further analysis of dependent variable; effect on health of the residents, it was observed that it varied significantly with

Table 4.24 : Analysis of Variance for Satisfaction Derived from Use of OBM in the Home by the Selected Respondents

Source of Variation	*Degree of Freedom*	*Sum of Squares*	*Mean of Squares*	*F Value*	*Significance Level*
Personal Variables					
Age	3.00	268.57	89.52	42.83	0.01
	196.00	409.19	2.09		
Educational	2.00	2.09	1.05	0.55	N.S.
Qualification	197.00	375.66	1.91		
Employment Status	1.00	9.49	9.49		
	198.00	6668.26	33.68	0.28	N.S.
Family Variables					
Family Size	2.00	23.07	11.54	49.09	0.01
	197.00	46.31	0.24		
Occupational Status	2.00	12.47	6.23	0.18	N.S.
	197.00	6665.29	33.83		
Family Income	2.00	60.60	30.30	9.68	0.01
	197.00	617.15	3.13		
Situational Variables					
Location of House	1.00	453.01	453.01	14.41	0.01
	198.00	6224.75	31.44		
Age of Building	1.00	3.00	3.00	9.38	0.01
Structure	198.00	63.19	0.32		
Occupancy Period	1.00	92.99	92.99	31.52	0.01
	198.00	584.76	2.95		

age (F = 4.92), family size (F = 53.65), family income (F = 2.8), age of the building structure (F = 4.56) and location of the house (F = 12.46). It was found that satisfaction derived not varied significantly with educational qualification, employment status, occupation of the family and occupancy period.

Therefore, hypothesis was rejected for age, family size, family income, location of the house, and age of the building structure and accepted for educational qualification, employment status, occupation of the family and occupancy period.

Table 4.25 : Analysis of Variance for effect on Health of the Residents by the Selected Respondents

Source of Variation With Knowledge	*Degree of Freedom*	*Sum of Squares*	*Mean of Squares*	*F Value*	*Significance Level*
Personal Variables					
Age	3.00	54.47	18.16	4.92	0.01
	196.00	724.41	3.69		
Educational	2.00	1.49	0.74	0.19	N.S.
Qualification	197.00	775.39	3.94		
Employment	1.00	0.00	0.00	0.00	N.S.
Status	198.00	2778.88	14.03		
Family Variables					
Family Size	2.00	69.21	34.61	53.65	0.01
	197.00	127.15	0.65		
Occupational	2.00	4.34	2.17	0.15	N.S.
Status	197.00	2769.16	14.06		
Family Income	2.00	21.52	10.76	2.80	0.05
	197.00	757.36	3.84		
Situational Variables					
Location of House	1.00	6.48	6.48	12.46	0.01
	198.00	103.15	0.52		
Age of Building	1.00	21.18	21.18	4.56	0.05
Structure	198.00	918.00	4.64		
Occupancy Period	1.00	0.53	0.53	0.14	N.S.
	198.00	757.70	3.83		

$H_{0\text{-}5}$: Temperature and humidity inside the home do not associated with extent of use of OBM in the residential constructions.

t-value (Table 4.26) revealed that there was significant difference at 1 per cent level between temperature inside the wooden and non-wooden houses. Thus, hypothesis was rejected. It could be inferred that there is difference in temperature of houses made up of wood and materials other than wood.

It was observed that t-value calculated was not significant

between extent of use of OBM in home for the wooden and non-wooden houses. Thus, hypothesis was accepted. It could be inferred that there is no difference in extent of use of OBM in houses made up of wood and materials other than wood, both were organic building materials varying in their sources, composition, properties and structures. (Table 4.26)

Table 4.26 : t- values showing difference between Homes with OBM and without OBM for Selected Variables

Variables	*Mean*	*t- values*	*Degree of Freedom*	*Significance Level*
Extent of use of OBM in Home	5.33 5.17	0.360413	10	N.S.
Temperature Inside House	15.65 20.01	4.31352	10	0.01
Humidity Inside House	43.21 42.42	0.314427	10	N.S.

It was also observed that t-value calculated (Table 4.26) was not significant between humidity inside house for the wooden and non-wooden houses. Thus, hypothesis was accepted. It could be inferred that there is no difference in humidity inside houses.

Further, on regression analysis it is clear from Figure 4.15 that temperature inside the houses changes linearly with extent of use of OBM in wooden as well as non-wooden houses. But the temperature range is higher in wooden houses than the non-wooden houses. It could be inferred that wood is a better OBM to be used in the hill areas where in winters, outside temperature decreases to a greater extent.

Figure 4.16 revealed the regression analysis of humidity inside the houses with extent of use of OBM in wooden and non-wooden houses. It had been shown that in wooden houses, the humidity changes in increasing order linearly with the change in extent of use of wood in the houses. But the reverse happened in the case of non-wooden houses. It could be concluded that the problem of dampness persists more in wooden houses.

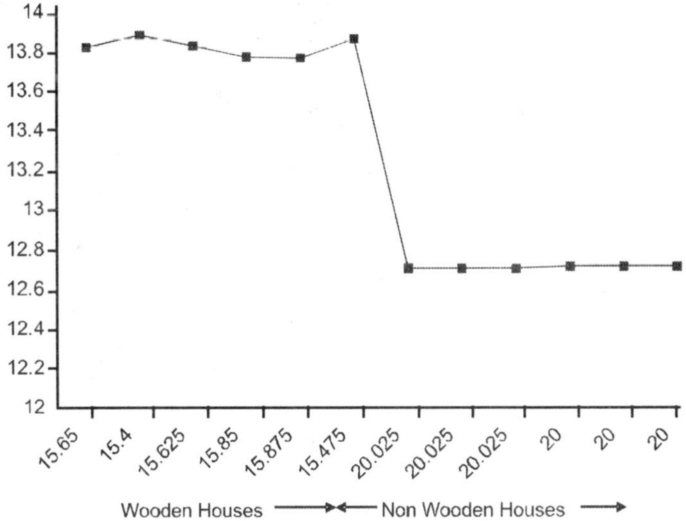

Figure 4.15 : Regression Analysis of Extent of Use of OBM with Temperature inside the House

Figure 4.16: Regression Analysis of Extent of Use with Humidity inside the House

$H_{0\text{-}0}$: Human performance in terms of short-term memory, attention/ concentration and work and fatigue do not have association with temperature and humidity inside the home.

It was observed that t-value calculated was not significant short-term memory between the respondents in homes of the wooden and non-wooden. Thus, hypothesis was accepted. It could be inferred that there is no difference in short-term memory of people in houses made up of wood and materials other than wood. (Table 4.27)

On the basis of the t-value calculated, no significant difference between attention/concentration of the respondents in the wooden and non-wooden houses. Thus, hypothesis was accepted. It could be inferred that there is no difference in attention/concentration in houses made up of wood and materials other than wood. (Table 4.27)

Table 4.27 : t- values Showing Difference Between Homes with OBM and without OBM for Selected Variables

Variables	*Mean*	*t- values*	*Degree of Freedom*	*Significance Level*
Short-Term Memory	0.976191 0.666667	0.020528	10	N.S.
Attention/Concentration	1.25 0.583333	0.168513	10	N.S.
Work and Fatigue	9 14.5	9.53782	10	0.01

t-value (Table 4.27) revealed that there was significant difference at 1 per cent level between work and fatigue inside the wooden and non-wooden houses. Thus, hypothesis was rejected. It could be inferred that there is difference in work and fatigue level of respondents in houses made up of wood and materials other than wood.

Figures 4.17 and 4.18 show regression analysis of short-term memory and attention/concentration values recorded for the respondents. Trend was same for the short term memory as well as attention/concentration. Values changed

Figure 4.17 : Regression Analysis of Short Term Memory in an Association with Temperature inside the House

Figure 4.18 : Regression Analysis of Attention/Concentration in an Association with Temperature inside the House

linearly with the temperature changes. But a clear difference was noted in the values for the selected performance parameters in wooden and non-wooden houses. The respondents residing in wooden houses performed better than the respondents living in the non-wooden houses.

Figure 4.19 showed the same trend between the relationship of temperature and work and fatigue. It meant the linear relationship between the performance and environment. But the case was *vice-versa* for the relationship in the performance of the respondents living in wooden and non-wooden houses. The respondents of non-wooden houses felt fatigue more than the fatigue felt by the respondents of wooden houses.

Results depicted in Figure 4.20 showed regression analysis of parameters of human performance (short-term memory, attention/concentration and work and fatigue) in association with parameter of environment (humidity) inside the wooden and non-wooden houses. It could be concluded from the graph that short-term memory changed linearly in relation to humidity. The values were constant for all the respondents and no marked difference was found in the short-term memory of the respondent living in two different types of home.

In case of attention/concentration of the respondents living in two different types of houses, difference was observed among the respondents on the basis of the construction material used. The attention level of the respondents was lower than the attention level of the respondents living in the wooden houses.

Work and fatigue values recorded for the respondents showed that there was not a much difference in the level of fatigue but the values were lower for the respondents living in the non-wooden houses.

FOLLOW UP ACTION

Knowledge refers to acquaintance with the facts and range of awareness or understanding. In other words, it implies a clear perception of something.

Figure 4.19 : Regression Analysis of Work and Fatigue in an Association with Temperature inside the House

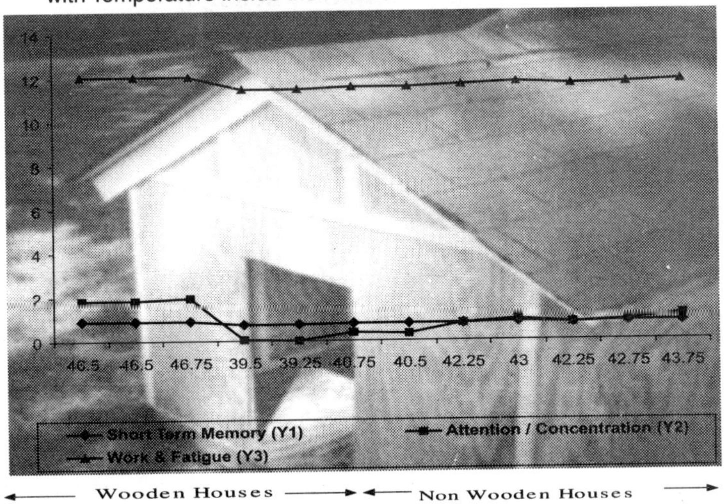

Figure 4.20 : Regression Analysis of Short Term Memory, Attention/ Concentration and Work and Fatigue in an Association with Humidity inside the House

During the investigation it was found that among the selected respondents most of them had low level of knowledge regarding organic building materials (Table 4.12a), which might hinder in living a safer and healthier life. Therefore a techno-kit on OBM was prepared by the investigator for disseminating knowledge regarding OBM and residential constructions, impact on the buildings and the health of the people living in these houses. Remedial measures to safeguard against the negative effects of OBM were also included. A sample of 33 respondents from the same population was selected to assess the efficacy of techno-kit on OBM prepared by the investigator.

Contents of the Techno-Kit (Communication Package)

- Organic Building Materials,
- Environmental Factors Affecting Indoor Housing Conditions,

Figure 4.20 : Development of Techno-Kit (Communication Package)

Media ⟶ Interactive

Message ⟶ Techno-kit on Organic Building Materials and Residential Constructions

Treatment ⟶ English

Experimental Site ⟶ Haldwani and Rudrapur

Respondents ⟶ 33

↓

Pre-Test (Low knowledge)

↓

Exposure

↓

Post Test I (Gain in knowledge)

↓

Retention

↓

Post Test II (Improvement in knowledge)

- Traditional Residential Constructions/State of Art in Uttaranchal,
- Health Problems due to Indoor Environment in Residential Buildings,
- Identification of Defective Symptoms/Deterio-ration in Residential Constructions,
- Remedial Measures to Safeguard Organic Building Materials,
- Measures to Control Indoor Problems in Resi-dential Constructions.

Part A: Pre-Exposure

The knowledge tool was given to the respondents and they were asked to write 'T' for true and 'F' for false answers. Thirty minutes time was given to each respondent to complete the tool. After thirty minutes it was collected back and scored to find out the pre-test score of each individual.

Table 4.27a: Level of Knowledge Regarding Organic Building Materials before Exposure (n=33)

S.No.	*Level of Knowledge*	*Scores*	*Respondents*	
			F	*%*
1	Low Level	102-135	30	90.91
2	Middle Level	136-170	3	9.09
3	High Level	171-204	00	00.00

Table 4.27a showed a poor level of knowledge by majority of the respondents (90.91 per cent) and high level of the knowledge by none of them.

Part B: Intervention Programme

An intervention programme was organized for the respondents. The respondents were given knowledge regarding "Organic Building Materials and Residential

Constructions" in the form of booklet. Besides this, html document was also used to impart the knowledge to the selected respondents. All the respondents were grouped in pairs. Total two hours of instruction was given to them, which started from the definition of the OBM. The level of understanding was checked by cross-questioning method with the participants. Their queries were satisfied with the help of suitable examples.

Part C: Gain in Knowledge (Post Exposure)

Gain in Knowledge

Knowledge is the total amount of information understood by an individual; it can be defined as a body of understood information as possessed by an individual. Gain in knowledge is any pre-post test change in person's cognitive learning behaviour resulting from a specific learning experience. In the present study gain in knowledge refers to the extra knowledge gain by the respondents after exposure to media. It was calculated by deducting pre-test scores from post-test scores.

Soon after the exposure of the respondents to intervention programme, second set of the knowledge test containing same questions was distributed and they were asked to write true or false for the answer. Thirty minutes time was given to them. After thirty minutes questionnaire was collected back and gain in knowledge was calculated.

Table 4.28 : Level of Knowledge Regarding Organic Building Materials after Exposure (n=33)

S.No.	*Level of Knowledge*	*Scores*	*Respondents*	
			F	*%*
1.	Low Level	102-135	00	00.00
2.	Middle Level	136-170	26	78.79
3.	High Level	171-204	7	21.21

Table 4.28 revealed that there was an increase in the knowledge of the respondents. Some of the respondents having poor level of knowledge regarding OBM moved upto middle level of the knowledge and those having middle level of knowledge moved upto higher level of knowledge after the intervention programme. Hence after about three-fourth of the respondents (78.79 per cent) showed middle level and 21 per cent showed higher level of the knowledge. None of them was in the category of poor level of the knowledge.

Part D: Post Exposure II or Retention of Message

The retention of message is the net amount of message remembered or recalled out of total message communicated at a particular time and situation. In this study retention was measured after 15 days of exposure. It was computed by deducting post-test I score from post-test score II.

Further, analysis of the scores was done by applying paired t-test and t-values shows a significant difference in the scores of the respondents during pre-exposure, after intervention programme and post-exposure (after a gap of 15 days). Hence it was concluded that the developed techno-kit helped in improvement of knowledge regarding OBM.

Table 4.29 : Level of Knowledge Regarding Organic Building Materials Showing Retention Level of the Message (n=33)

S.No.	*Level of Knowledge*	*Scores*	*Respondents*	
			F	*%*
1.	Low Level	102-135	01	3.03
2.	Middle Level	136-170	32	96.97
3.	High Level	171-204	00	00.00

It is clear from Table 4.29 that majority of the respondents possessed middle level of the knowledge after the gap of 15 days. It meant that there was retention of knowledge in the respondents.

Table 4.30 : Values of Paired t-test Showing Difference Between Knowle dge Level of the Selected Respondents before and afterExposure (retention) to the Techno-kit Developed

Variables	*Mean*	*t- values*	*Degree of Freedom*	*Significance Level*
Knowledge Level				
Before Exposure	113.05	8.57	64	0.01
After Exposure	142.97			

Table 4.30 showed t-test with a highly significant values for before and after exposure of techno-kit developed for the enhancement in knowledge level of the respondents regarding organic building materials. It could be concluded from the significant relationship that there was a definite gain in knowledge of the respondents after using the techno-kit developed for the purpose of increasing awareness among the people about OBM and their proper uses in residential constructions.

5 Summary and Conclusions

Building materials are most important materials for human beings. Since prehistoric times man has been using naturally available organic materials for his requirements. In India, animal (bovine) dung has been used to improve the properties of clays. Grasses have been used to provide protection from sun and rain (thatch). Naturally available bees-wax, lac and oils have been used to water proof pots and ceramics. Gradually, as the man's knowledge increased, various oils were processed to make paints and varnishes. Similarly, casein, starches were modified to obtain adhesives.

Use of wood in buildings, construction and decoration is still considered of higher aesthetic value than other competing material. With the increasing emphasis on environment protection and environment friendly technologies, it has become immensely important to work towards development of wood substitutes. In present period, a number of organic substances were synthesized many of organic substances present in nature and also produced thousands of substances that do not occur in nature and plastics/polymers are on such group of substances. Polymers are becoming day by day important as organic building materials due to their binding and insulation characteristics. Polymers are expensive materials so some filler like particulates, agro-wastes, industrial wastes, fibres, whiskers are added to formulate composite building materials.

Organic building materials are widely used as structural engineering materials for indoor and outdoor applications. In exterior use, wood is subjected to varying environmental conditions resulting in physical deterioration, discolouration, surface roughening, cracking and damages of the microstructure. Weathering affects physical and mechanical properties of wood and also results in premature coating failure. Infestation of pests also results underneath clear finishes, affects coating adhesion and degradates service life of the building materials. Plastics being organic in nature are prone to attack UV present in sun-light and other weathering elements such as temperature variation, moisture, wind, dust, ozone, etc. These materials and environmental effects together make an indoor climate to be lived in a house.

Physical environment provided by a house has a profound effect on the performance of physical tasks. It can also affect mental task performance. Cold causes peripheral vasoconstriction, shivering, impaired neural conduction and poorer muscular control, all of which may have effects, such as longer reaction time, which may appear to be of psychological nature. Low relative humidity (less than 40 per cent) may also increase the risk of respiratory infection. (Bredger, 1995)

There is a less or negligible documentation about the relationship among Organic Building Materials (OBM), housing conditions in OBM houses, health and human behaviour. Therefore, a need was felt to conduct a study on residences made from organic building materials in order to search a link of the residences with physiological, physical and mental health issues.

Objectives

1. To make an inventory of organic building materials (OBM) available and their use in residential constructions.
2. To find out extent of use of OBM in residential constructions.

3. To assess problems experienced in care and maintenance in the selected residential constructions.
4. To find out the health problems perceived by the residents due to use of OBM.
5. To ascertain the knowledge and satisfaction level of residents regarding OBM.
6. To assess level of human performance in the selected residential buildings with OBM constructions.
7. To develop an educational material on increasing awareness regarding proper use of OBM.

Delimitations

1. The study will be limited to two districts of Uttaranchal, namely :
   (c) Nainital
   (d) Udham Singh Nagar.

2. The study will be limited to 200 residents comprising 100 residents in each district.
3. The experiment will be limited to assess :

   (e) Mental performance (memory, attention and mental fatigue),
   (f) Indoor environment (temperature and humidity).

Hypothesis

H_1: Knowledge regarding OBM, extent of use of OBM in home and problems faced in care and maintenance are associated with personal variables, family variables and situational variables.

H_2: There is an inter-relationship among knowledge regarding OBM, extent of use of OBM in home and problems faced in its care and maintenance.

H_3: Knowledge regarding OBM, extent of use of OBM in home and problems faced in care and maintenance of the houses are associated with satisfaction derived from use of OBM and effect on health of the residents.

H_4: Satisfaction derived from use of OBM and effect on health of the residents has an association with personal variables, family variables and situational variables.

H_5: Temperature and humidity inside the home is associated with extent of use of OBM in the residential constructions.

H_6: Human performance in terms of short-term memory, attention/concentration and work and fatigue has an association with temperature and humidity inside the home.

Assumption

Uttaranchal is an organic state and organic building materials are used in residential constructions.

Methodology

Research Design

Exploratory-cum-Experimental research design was planned to describe, to correlate and to measure housing conditions due to use of organic building materials and psychological behaviour of residents.

Sampling Design and Locale of the Study

Multistage purposive-cum-random sampling design was adopted to select 200 residential buildings in Uttaranchal.

Development of the Tool and Data Collection

To record information in the interview schedule personal interview method is appropriate. An interview schedule having descriptive statements, observation charts and experiment sheets was developed to collect subjective as well as experimental data during face to face interview with residents.

To measure the level of knowledge of the respondents regarding quality of environment, an attempt has been made to develop a knowledge test in view of the fact that it plays an important role in achieving and maintaining quality of the environment in the residential constructions.

A three point Likert type scale was developed to assess satisfaction derived from use of OBM in residential constructions.

To assess level of human performance in the selected residential buildings with OBM constructions, it was felt necessary to conduct experiments on certain psychological aspects and indoor environment of the residents, in terms of short-term memory, work and fatigue, attention/concentration, temperature and humidity. The listed parameters were recorded with standardized tests and equipments.

Data Analysis

Descriptive as well as relational statistics were used to analyze the data in the study. Pearson's product moment coefficient of correlation, t-test, regression analysis and Analysis of Variance (ANOVA) were employed to test the hypothesis formulated for the present study.

Major Findings of the Study

Personal Profile of the Respondents

The mean age of the respondents was about 36 years with a standard deviation of ± 9 years. It revealed that they were having a settled life and living in a particular house for many years. None of them was found to be illiterate. About 88 per cent were unemployed respondents, which mean they were spending most of the hours in their houses thus, having a close contact with building materials used in their homes for longer duration than other members of their families.

Demographic Profile of the Respondents

Among the respondents half of them belonged to service class families and a little less than half of them were from business class families having an average income of about Rs. 9,400 with a standard deviation of Rs. ± 5826.92. It implied that some of them can afford a house of their own but many of them were living in rented houses.

General Information about the Houses of the Respondents

Houses selected for the study were in hills as well as plain topographic areas to minimize biasness of results due to geographical factors. The residences were mostly *pucca* houses and thus built of natural as well as synthetic organic building materials. Through many generations of use, people have found ways of getting around some of the limitations of naturally occurring organic construction materials. In addition to improving natural materials, technologies have developed many synthetic polymers, which are important in current constructions (Merritt, 1986) and make the houses *pucca*. The residents were selected having resided in their houses atleast for five years so that effect of the OBM can better be perceived and a cause effect relationship could be established between the OBM and health of the residents. About 72 per cent houses were having a life of atleast ten years. It helped in assessment of defective problems/ symptoms in due course of time due to degenerative changes and also minimized effect of volatile organic compounds emitting out of newly built OBM residences.

General Living Habits of thc Respondents

The residences were selected on the basis of use of clear fuel. Most of the selected respondents reported that they are using either LPG or electricity or both for lighting as well as cooking purposes. Smokers were found only in twenty per cent of the houses. Most of the respondents were spending their 13-24 hours of time per day in their homes. Townsend *et al.* in 1988 also recommended that 'Housing conditions are associated with health status in a variety of ways'. The conditions were found to be very much suitable to assess effect of OBM on the residents.

Organic Building Materials and Their Sources

Building materials used in construction and during renovation were classified under six categories and then it was noted down that the materials were available in their vicinity easily or not. It was found that materials used for masonry purposes were available only in few areas and people have to bring them from far off places. OBM like wood, plastics, roofing materials, sealants, and adhesives are available in nearby markets. But people are buying protective and decorative finishes and materials used for reinforcement from far off places, sometimes from other districts and states, too.

Extent of Use of Organic Building Materials

Wood was the material used by 17.50 per cent residents in all the areas for doors, windows, ventilators, cupboards and half of the respondents (for floors, roofs, working counters and staircases) whereas, about 44 per cent of them used it in most of the areas and about 38.50 per cent of them used it for some of the areas. Stone was also used as basic material for roof, cupboards, walls and working counters by about half of the respondents.

Care and Maintenance in the Residential Constructions

The data showed that most of the care and maintenance was done by the respondents on their own. More than 90 minutes per month were reported for cleaning of cupboards by little less than of the respondents (44 per cent). Roofs and walls requiring least maintenance was reported by about one third of the respondents (29.50 per cent) and floors were cleaned daily by more than a half of the respondents (69.50 per cent).

Cost involved in the cleaning and maintenance was reported least (Rs. 0-500 per month) in cupboards by 91 per cent of the respondents and highest (Rs. 1001 and above) in the cleaning of the floors by 11.50 per cent of the respondents.

Assessment of Problems Experienced in Care and Maintenance

In due course of time several defective symptoms were observed in the houses like deformity, smell, dampness, flaking off, shorter life, allergy, corrosion, vegetative growth, fire ignition, dust release, noise, fumes, termite, mold growth, reaction with water, reaction with food materials and heating were the problems experienced by the residents in their homes. Among these problems mostly reported were deformity in walls by 75 per cent of the respondents, dampness in walls by 77.50 per cent and in roof by 62.50 per cent of the respondents, flaking off in walls by 65 per cent of them, dust release from doors, windows and ventilators by about 45 per cent of them, problem of termite in cupboards by about one third and heating up of roof was reported by about 42.50 per cent of the respondents.

Health Problems Perceived due to use of Organic Building Materials

Various health symptoms were highly perceived by

95 per cent of the respondents as an effect of the OBM used in their houses. Among them lethargy (often felt by 45 per cent respondents) was ranked first, fatigue (often felt by 45 per cent respondents) second and symptoms of humidified fever (often felt by 40 per cent respondents) as third.

Among building related health syndromes one fourth of them reported asthma like symptoms as major problem. Legionnaire's disease was also reported as a major problem by 7.50 per cent of them. Extreme dust sensitivity was reported as a major problem by 25 per cent of the respondents.

Assessment of Knowledge and Satisfaction Level regarding Organic Building Materials

Among the selected respondents most of them i.e. about 96.50 per cent showed a low level of knowledge regarding OBM used in their houses and a very few of them reflected middle level (3.50 per cent).

As per satisfaction OBM were ranked first on safety and care and maintenance, second on cost, third on function/ purpose and lastly on no health effects.

Parameters of Human Performance (Short-term memory, attention/concentration, work and fatigue)

The numbers of mistakes done by the respondents living in houses completely build up of natural OBM i.e. wood was lower than the respondents living in non-wooden houses.

The poorer concentration level was shown by the respondents living in non-wooden houses than the wooden houses.

The number of sums done by the respondents living in the non-wooden houses was more than the sums done by the respondents living in wooden houses. But, number of mistakes performed by the respondents was more by the respondents living in the wooden houses were more than the sums done by the respondents living in non-wooden houses. It shows that level of fatigue was reflected more by the respondents living in non-wooden houses.

Parameters of Indoor Environment (Temperature and Humidity)

A clear difference was found in the temperature and humidity in the selected group of houses. The percentage increase in temperature from outdoor to indoor environment was more in non-wooden houses than the wooden houses. But the results were *vice-versa* for the relative humidity.

Relationships among the Variables

In the present study, findings of the analysis confirmed that the knowledge regarding OBM of the respondents varied significantly with age, educational qualification, employment status, occupational status and location of house, which indicated that the knowledge varied due to these variables. Family income, family size, occupancy period and age of building structure which were found to be non-significant.

Extent of use of OBM in home varied significantly with age of the respondent, employment status and occupancy period and age of building structure and not found significantly associated with educational qualification, occupational status, family size, family income, location of house

Problems faced in care and maintenance of the home showed a significant variation with occupational status, family income and age of building structure and not found significant variation with age, educational qualification, employment status, family size, location of the house and occupancy period.

Significant relationship was observed between knowledge regarding OBM and extent of use of OBM in home. Whereas, relationship of extent of use of OBM in home and problems faced in its care and maintenance; knowledge regarding OBM and problems faced in its care and maintenance was found non-significant.

The relationship was found significant for knowledge regarding OBM and satisfaction derived from use of OBM, knowledge regarding OBM and effect on health and extent of use of OBM in home and satisfaction derived from use of OBM. Non-significant values were observed for association among extent of use of OBM in home and effect on health, problems faced in care and maintenance of the houses and satisfaction derived from use of OBM and problems faced in care and maintenance of the houses and effect on health.

Satisfaction derived from use of OBM in the home varied significantly with educational qualification, employment status and occupation of the family and did not vary with age, family size, family income, location of the house, occupancy period and age of the building structure.

Effect on health of the residents, it was observed that it varied significantly with educational qualification, employment status, occupation of the family and occupancy period and did not vary with age, family size, family income, location of the house, and age of the building structure.

Extent of use of OBM and humidity inside houses varied significantly for the wooden houses and non-wooden houses. However, it did not vary significantly for temperature inside houses.

Among human performance, work and fatigue did not vary significantly for the wooden and non-wooden houses but varied for short-term memory an attention/ concentration.

Follow up Action

There was a gain in knowledge of the respondents after using the techno-kit (communication package) developed for the purpose of increasing awareness among the people about OBM and their proper uses in residential constructions.

Conclusions

On the basis of the present investigation following conclusions are delineated:

- About half of the respondents belonged to service class families and a little less than half of them were from business class families not in a condition to afford a house of their own but many of them were living in rented houses.
- The residences were mostly *pucca* houses and built of natural as well as synthetic organic building materials.
- Materials used for masonry purposes were available only in few areas and people had to bring them from far off places. OBM like wood, plastics, roofing materials, sealants, and adhesives were available in nearby markets. But people are buying protective and decorative finishes and materials used for reinforcement from far off places, sometimes from markets of other districts and states, too.
- Wood was the mostly used organic building material in all the areas of the house in the hilly areas. But in plains, other organic materials were also being used due to availability, geographical conditions and residential needs.
- Care and maintenance of the house required a lot of time, energy and money. Roofs and walls required least maintenance and floor required the utmost care, cleaning and maintenance.
- Deformity in walls, dampness, flaking off, dust release, termite and heating up were the problems

experienced/observed in the houses. The problems of rot, cracking, stains, long filament growth and small holes were prominent in wooden houses and problem of flaking was more in the non-wooden houses.

- Lethargy, fatigue and symptoms of humidified fever were the main health symptoms reported by the respondents. Syndromes such as asthma like symptoms and extreme dust sensitivity were also reported by the respondents.
- Among the selected respondents most of them showed a low level of knowledge regarding OBM used in their houses and a very few of them reflected middle level of knowledge.
- As per satisfaction OBM were ranked first on safety, care and maintenance, second on cost, third on function/purpose and they felt no health effects due to OBM.
- Short-term memory of the respondents living in houses completely build up of natural OBM i.e. wood was higher than the respondents living in non-wooden houses.
- The poor concentration level was shown by the respondents living in non-wooden houses.
- The level of fatigue was felt more by the respondents living in non-wooden houses than the wooden houses.
- The percentage increase in temperature from outdoor to indoor environment was more in non-wooden houses than the wooden houses. But the results were *vice-versa* for the relative humidity.
- There is association of the knowledge regarding OBM of the respondents with age, educational qualification, employment status, occupational status and location of house.
- Extent of use of OBM in home is associated with

educational qualification, occupational status, family size, family income, location of house.

- Problems faced in care and maintenance of the home have a relationship with age, educational qualification, employment status, family size, location of the house and occupancy period.
- There is a relationship among extent of use of OBM in home and problems faced in its care and maintenance; knowledge regarding OBM and problems faced in its care and maintenance.
- There is an association among the variables; extent of use of OBM in home and effect on health, problems faced in care and maintenance of the houses and satisfaction derived from use of OBM and problems faced in care and maintenance of the houses and effect on health.
- Age of the building structure has an association with age, family size, family income, location of the house, occupancy period.
- The temperature inside the houses changes linearly with extent of use of OBM in wooden as well as non-wooden houses. But the temperature range is higher in wooden houses than the non-wooden houses. Therefore, wood is a better OBM to be used in the hill areas wherein winters, outside temperature decreases to a greater extent.
- In wooden houses, the humidity increases linearly with the extent of use of wood in the houses. But the reverse happened in the case of non-wooden houses. Thus the problem of dampness persists more in wooden houses.
- The respondents residing in wooden houses performed better than the respondents living in the non wooden houses in terms of short-term memory as well as attention/concentration.
- The respondents of non-wooden houses felt fatigue

more than the fatigue felt by the respondents of wooden houses.

- There was no marked difference in the short-term memory of the respondent living in two different types of home in relation to humidity.
- The attention level of the respondents living in non-wooden houses was lower than the attention level of the respondents living in the wooden houses.
- There was not a much difference in the level of fatigue but the values were lower for the respondents living in the non-wooden houses.
- A significant gain in knowledge level regarding OBM was found after administration of the intervention package on OBM and residential constructions.

Implications of the Study

The findings of the investigation brought out a number of important implications:

The results of the investigation showed that the respondents lacked knowledge regarding organic building materials, their effects on health and how to maintain the good quality of the indoor environment comprising of building materials.

- From the findings, it was revealed that the respondents had poor level of knowledge before the follow up of the study. Thus awareness programmes on proper use of organic building materials need to be organized.
- It was found that wood is a widely used organic building material in the area due to reasons of its applicability, durability and aestheticy in the houses. Wood is subjected to bio-deterioration, infestation of pests and dampness. Thus, there is a need to synthesize alternative building materials to replace the wood in certain parts.
- The architects, engineers and researchers need to develop ways of increasing the efficiency of the OBM in the houses and thereby increase the level of satisfaction deriving from the use of the OBM.

Recommendations for Future Research

Organic building material is comparatively an emerging field and a lot of further research and investigation related to various aspects is required. A few suggestions for future research are submitted as under:

- The same study with larger sample and comparison of the parameters taken for the study in different season can be conducted.
- A study on comparison between effects of OBM in the hill areas and plains can be carried out.
- Effect of environmental parameters other than temperature and humidity along with the OBM can be studied.
- Infestation of various pathological tests on building materials is an interesting area where lot of work could be done.
- Experiments can be conducted with the laboratory testing of allergens arising due to OBM in the indoor environment.
- Relationship of particular health syndromes and various housing conditions due to OBM could be explored.
- Development of various communication media on building materials and their efficacy can be computed for effectiveness of awareness gene-ration programmes regarding OBM.

ANNEXURE-1

PART I
Interview Schedule

General Information

1. Name of the Respondent:
2. Address:
3. Profile of Family Members:

S. No.	Member	M/F	Relationship To Respondent	Age (yrs)	Educational Qualification	Employment	Income (Rs.)

4. Location of the House
   (a) Hills (b) Plains
5. Type of the House
   (a) *Kuccha* (c) Semi-*pucca*
   (b) *Pucca* (d) Wooden
6. Age of the Structure (Years)
   (a) 5 - 10 (b) More than 10
7. Occupancy Period (Years)
   (a) 5 - 10 (b) More than 10
8. Type of Fuel use for Cooking
   (a) Wood and Dung Cakes (c) Kerosene
   (b) LPG (d) Electricity
   (e) Any other
9. Is anyone a Smoker in the House?
   (a) Yes (b) No

10. Period of Occupancy in House per day

S. No	Member	Child/Adult	Period (min)

CARE AND MAINTENANCE OF HOME

1. Please, specify the details of cleaning and care in the home.

Room	*Area*	*Person Involved*			*Time Taken (min)*	*Frequency of Care*	*Cost Involved (Rs.)*
		Adult	Child	Servant			
Living Room	Roof Floor Walls Doors, Windows and Ventilators Cupboards						
Bed-Room	Roof Floor Walls Doors, Windows and Ventilators Cupboards						
Kitchen	Roof Floor Walls Doors, Windows and Ventilators Cupboards Sink Working Counters						

(Contd...)

(contd...)

Store-room	Roof Floor Walls Doors, Windows and Ventilators Cupboards and built in Shelves						
Bath-room	Roof and Walls Floor Doors and Ventilators Bathtub and Wash-basin Cupboards						
Angan	Floor Walls Doors Pots						
Stair-cases	Steps Side Support Roof						

2. Please specify the details of repair in the home.

Room	*Area*	*Type of Repaired*		*Frequency of Repair (months)*	*Cost Involved (Rs.)*
		Own	*Hired*		
Living Room	Roof Floor Walls Doors, Windows and Ventilators Cupboards Electric fitting				
Bed Room	Roof Floor Walls Doors,				

(Contd...)

(Contd...)

	Windows and Ventilators				
	Cupboards				
	Electric fitting				
Kitchen	Roof				
	Floor				
	Walls				
	Doors, Windows and Ventilators				
	Cupboards				
	Sink				
	Working Counters				
	Electric fitting				
	Plumbing				
	Drainage				
Store-room	Roof				
	Floor				
	Walls				
	Doors, Windows and Ventilators				
	Cupboards & Built in Shelves				
	Electric fitting				
Bath-room	Roof and walls				
	Floor				
	Doors and Ventilators				
	Bathtub and Washbasin				
	Cupboards				
	Electric fitting				
	Water fitting				
	Drainage				
Angan	Floor				
	Walls				
	Doors				
	Pots				
Stair-cases	Steps				
	Side support				
	Roof				

3. Sources of building materials at the time of construction and during renovation. (C = Construction, R = Renovation)

S. No	Used in Area	Name of Material		Name of the Source		Year of Purchase		Cost (Rs.)	
		R	C	R	C	R	C	R	C
1.	Floor								
2.	Roof								
3.	Walls								
4.	Doors								
5.	Windows								
6.	Ventilator								
7.	Cupboard								
8.	Plumbing								
9.	Electric fitting								
10.	Work Counters								
11.	Bath Accessories								

4. Please specify extent of use of following organic building materials in your home

Sr. No.	OBM	Extent of Use					
		All Areas		Most of Areas		Some Areas	
		Yes	No	Yes	No	Yes	No
1.	Wood and its Products						
2.	Plastic Products						
3.	Asphalt						
4.	Bitumen						
5.	Resins/Adhesives						

5. Is there any finish/technique adopted in the home to withstand accidents?

Sr. No.	Area	Aspect Termite	Fire	Earth-quake	Electric Shock	Moisture (Dampness)	Any Other
1.	Entire House						
2.	Specific Area						
(i)	Living Room						
(ii)	Bed Room						
(iii)	Kitchen						
(iv)	Store Room						
(v)	Bathroom						
(vi)	Staircases						
(vii)	Verandah						
(viii)	Any Other						

6.Do you observe following problems in the areas of home where OBM have been used?

Sr. No.	Problem	Area Walls	Roof	Doors	Windows	Floor	Cupboard	Remarks
1.	Deformity							
2.	Smell							
3.	Dampness							
4.	Flaking off							
5.	Shorter life							
6.	Allergy							
7.	Corrosion							
8.	Vegetative Growth							
9.	Fire Ignition							
10.	Dust Release							
11.	Noise							
12.	Fumes							
13.	Termite							
14.	Mold Growth							
15.	Reaction with Water							
16.	Reaction with Food Materials							
17.	Heats Up							

Health Problems Perceived by the Residents

1. Do you feel any of the following health symptoms? If yes, how frequently?

Sr. No.	Problems	Often	Sometimes	Never
1	Sneezing			
2	Dizziness			
3	Cough			
4	Headache			
5	Nausea			
6	Fatigue			
7	Excitement			
8	Eye Irritation			
9	Effect on Hearing			

(Contd...)

(Contd...)

10 Skin Irritation			
11 Effect on Visibility			
12 Throat Irritation			
13 Mental Fatigue			
14 Chest Tightness			
15 Shortness of Breath			
16 Wheeze			
17 Nose Bleeds			
18 Dry Skin			
19 Skin Rash			
20 Lethargy			
21 Symptoms of Humidifier Fever			

2. State the illness affected by you in this home (last 5 years).

Sr. No.	*Health Problem*	*Major Problem*	*Minor Problem*	*No Problem*
A.	*Sick Building Syndrome*			
	- Symptoms of eye irritation			
	- Symptoms of throat irritation			
	- Symptoms of nose irritation			
	- Symptoms of mucosa of skin			
	- Mental fatigue			
	- Arythema			
B.	*Building Related illness*			
	- Asthama like symptoms			
	- Legionnair's disease			
	- Hyper sensitivity			
	- Humidifier fever			
C.	*Multiple Chemical Sensitivity*			
	- Extreme dust sensitivity			
	- Chronic fatigue			
	- Nausea			
	- Headache			
D.	*Any other (specify)*			

PART II - OBSERVATION-CUM-INTERVIEW SHEET

1. Existing Materials used in Construction of the Home

Room	*Area*	*Basic Material*	*Other Material*	*Finish*	*Material Used*
Living Room	Roof				
	Floor				
	Walls				
	Doors, Windows and Ventilators				
	Cupboards				
	Electric fitting				
Bed Room	Roof				
	Floor				
	Walls				
	Doors, Windows and Ventilators				
	Cupboards				
	Electric fitting				
Kitchen	Roof				
	Floor				
	Walls				
	Doors, Windows and Ventilators				
	Cupboards				
	Sink				
	Working Counters				
	Electric fitting				
	Plumbing				
Store-room	Roof				
	Floor				
	Walls				
	Doors, Windows				

(Contd...)

(Contd...)

	and Ventilators Cupboards and Built in Shelves Electric fitting				
Bath-room	Roof and Walls Floor Doors and Ventilators Bathtub and Washbasin Cupboards Electric fitting Plumbing				
Angan	Floor Walls Doors Pots				
Stair cases	Steps Side Support Roof				

2. Checklist of defective symptoms/problems in home.

Sr. No.	*Area*	*Defective Symptom*	*Yes*	*No*
1.	Roof	Rot Splits Granular surface Crumbled on surface Loosen pavings Dampness No grating Bubbles on surface Dirt Stains Infestation		
2.	Walls	Cracks Rot Twisted/Curled Dirty Spots Fractured		

(Contd...)

(Contd...)

	Dampness		
	Dry dirty patch		
	Sagging timber lining		
	Damp rising on internal walls		
3. Floors and Staircases	Rot		
(Timber)	Board crack underfoot		
	White spongy under floor covering		
	Bay dips outward		
	Stains		
	Long filament growth		
	1st floor unstable under foot cracks		
	Olive green or brown fruiting body on surfaces		
	Squeaks the staircases		
	Tread fall away		
	Small holes		
	Dirt		
	Saw dust.		
4. Internal finishes			
A. Plaster	Crack		
	Soft and Crumbly		
	Dry and Crumbly		
	Dampness		
	Bulging		
	Pinholes in joinery		
	Blister or small crater		
B. Painting	Bittiness		
	Blooming		
	Cissing		
	Drying trouble		
	Grinning		
	Mould		
	Shriveling		
	Bleeding		
	Brush marks		
	Crazing		
	Efflorescence		
	Loss of gloss		
	Poor opacity		
	Saponification		
	Blistoring		
	Chalking		

(Contd...)

(Contd...)

5. Services	Running Flaking Misses Sheeriness Leakage Noisy Encrustation Fungus Water stain Supply sluggish Lack of temp. Excessive joints Spots Smell of heating		

PART III - Experiments for Assessment of Human Performance

EXPERIMENT SHEET NO. 1

Experiment : Short-term Memory
Name : ________________
Subject : ________________
Experimenter :________________

Answer	*Stimulus*	*Interfering Task*	*Answer*	*Stimulus*	*Interfering Task*
______	1385	Fruit	______	7278	Cities
______	326579	Colours	______	2563456	Colours
______	54	Cities	______	4	Animals
______	83987	Animals	______	643	Fruit
______	445	Colours	______	644523	Animals
______	3	Fruit	______	326	Cities
______	7835882	Animals	______	93	Colours
______	965342	Cities	______	3454572	Fruit
______	24	Animals	______	5	Colours
______	272789	Fruit	______	56391	Fruit
______	9758	Colours	______	12511	Cities

(Contd...)

(Contd...)

______	7	Cities	______	4678	Animals
______	125	Animals			
______	76	Fruit			
______	4553245	Cities			
______	34521	Colours			

EXPERIMENT SHEET NO. 2

Experiment : Attention/Concentration

Subject : ____________________

Experimenter: ____________________

Individual	*No. of Times Attention Wanders*	
	Series 1	*Series 2*

EXPERIMENT SHEET NO. 3

Experiment : Work and Fatigue

Time: 30 minutes

Subject : ____________________

Experimenter: ____________________

Number Announced @ 30 sec	*Consecutive Sums (Adding 2,3,4,5, etc.)*	*Mistakes*

KNOWLEDGE SCALE

Please put tick mark against each answer as yes, no or don't know.

S.No.	*Item/Statement*	*Yes*	*No*	*Don't know*
A	*Use of OBM in home dates back to*			
1	Period of Harappa and Mohanjodaro			
2	1800s			
3	1900s			
4	Very recent			
5	Not known			
B	*Do you know OBM is made up of:*			
1	Hydrocarbons			
2	Recycled matter			
3	Wastes			
4	Sulphur, Nitrogen & O_2 derivatives			
5	All of the above			
C	*OBM are the materials which are always:*			
1	Eco-friendly			
2	Reusable			
3	Harmful to residents			
4	Not harmful to residents			
5	None of the above			
D	*OBM used in home, namely are:*			
1	Wood			
2	Clay			
3	Plastics			
4	Bitumen			
5	Paints			
6	All of the above			
E	*OBM originates from:*			
1	Animal origin			
2	Plant origin			
3	Wastes			
4	Chemicals			
5	All of the above			
F	*All OBM releases:*			
1	Fumes			

(Contd...)

(Contd...)

2 Odors			
3 Dust particles			
4 Volatile organic compounds			
5 None of the above			
G OBM are resistant to :			
1 Fire			
2 Earthquakes			
3 Heat			
4 Sound			
5 Termite			
6 Moisture			
7 Not necessarily from the above			
H OBM can only be used in :			
1 Homes			
2 Offices			
3 Schools			
4 Very modern and sophisticated homes			
5 All of the above			
I OBM in construction may be used for purpose of :			
1 Cost effectiveness			
2 Ease of care and maintenance			
3 Safety standards			
4 Aesthetic value			
5 Better health aspects			
6 All of the above			
J OBM availability is resumed with :			
1 Research institutions			
2 Big cities			
3 Innovative builders			
4 All hardware shops			
K Area(s) of OBM use in constructions : are/is			
1 Plinth			
2 Main structure			
3 Plumbing			
4 Electric fittings			
5 Built-in-cupboards and counters			
6 Paints and finishes			
7 All of the above			

(Contd...)

(Contd...)

L Energy used in temperature regulation in buildings of OBM is :			
1 Increased 2 Decreased 3 Depends on requirement			
M All OBM used creates :			
1 Deformity on doors 2 Flakes on walls and doors 3 Generation of fumes 4 Allergic agents 5 None of the above			
N OBM used in homes could add to :			
1 Air pollution 2 Water pollution 3 Thermal pollution 4 Noise pollution 5 All of the above			
O OBM could be improved to :			
1 Earthquake resistance 2 Fire resistance 3 Electric shock resistance 4 Damp proofing 5 Termite resistance 6 All of the above 7 None of the above			
P *Building related illness is :*			
1 Asthma like symptoms 2 Legionnaire's disease 3 Hypersensitivity 4 Humidifier fever 5 Cancer 6 All of the above			
Q Sick building syndrome aroused from building materials may lead to :			
1 Change in biological status of residents 2 Change in psychological status of residents 3 Change in mental level 4 All of the above			

(Contd...)

(contd...)

5 None of the above			
R Organic polymers include :			
1 Plastics, fibres, natural and synthetic rubber 2 Ceramic and glasses 3 Metal and alloys 4 Wood only 5 1 and 4 6 2 and 3			
S Housing environment indicating building materials affects the residents in terms of :			
1 Mental performance 2 Physiological performance 3 Physical performance 4 All of the above 5 None of the above			

SATISFACTION SCALE

Please put a tick mark against each statement as per your perception

S. No.	*Item/Statement*	*Highly Satisfactory*	*Satisfactory*	*Not Satisfactory*
A	*COST*			
1.	Cost of OBM at initial construction			
2.	Cost of OBM at time of renovation/repair			
3.	Cost involved in cleaning			
4.	Cost involved in heating of home			
5.	Cost involved in cooling of home			
6.	Cost involved in transportation of products			

(Contd...)

(Contd...)

B CARE AND MAINTENANCE			
1 Number of persons needed to be involved while cleaning			
2 Frequency of care to be done			
3 Time involved in cleaning			
4 Time involved in repair			
C FUNCTION/PURPOSE			
1 Heating in winters			
2 Cooling in summers			
3 Noise control			
4 Durability			
5 Strength			
6 Damp proofing			
7 Light in weight			
8 Aestheticity			
9 Fire proofing			
10 Dust control			
D SAFETY			
1 Electric shock proof			
2 Damp proof			
3 Earthquake resistant			
4 Fire proof			
5 Termite proof			
6 Allergy level			
7 Chemical reactions			
E HEALTH EFFECTS			
Respondents experienced no effect regarding :			
1 Skin allergies			
2 Bad odors			
3 Eye irritation			
4 Respiratory problems			
5 Fatigue or activeness			
6 Throat infection			
7 Headache			
8 Hypersensitivity			
9 Chemical reactions			

ANNEXURE-2

Short-Term Memory

Problem

It is a common experience that numbers are difficult to remember. It has been shown (Peterson & Peterson, 1959) that short-term memory decays rapidly. However, the subject must be occupied in some other task, so as to prevent rehearsal.

Procedure

The E will read a number, then a category name viz. fruits, colours, cities or animals. The subject first must give three examples of the category, and then try to repeat the number. His answer is scored as correct or wrong. The digits are read evenly, one each second, then the category name is given in rhythm. The subject must give examples of the category immediately, with no pause to rehearse the number. (Ost, 1969)

Vigilance Test for Attention/ Concentration

Problem

To discover number of times attention wanders and to find out conditions which help concentration or attention.

Materials

Pen or pencil, stop clock.

Prodcedure

Give instructions to S: 'Look at your pencil. Concentrate your attention upon it for one min. When your attention wanders from the object indicate by a movement of your left hand.' E notes down the number of times attention wanders during the one minute period.

In the second series give the following instructions. 'Look at the pencil. Think about its size, colour, material, with which it is made, flaws in the making, its uses, etc. Indicate as before when attention wanders.' E notes down the number of times attention wanders during the one minute period.

Find the number of time attention wanders in the first series and in the second series. Note the difference. Account for this difference, taking also into account the introspective report of S. collect the data for whole sample. Find the mean and S.D. for the two series and calculate the reliability of the difference. State the law of attention based on this work. (Kuppuswamy, 1954).

Work and Fatigue in Semi-Simplicity Activity

Problem

To measure continuous thinking work and its change, especially changes by fatigue.

Materials

Tables of numbers in vertical column for cumulative adding

Procedure

Subject (S) is to be comfortably seated in a quit room. Experimenter (E) is to pronounce aloud a number. S is immediately asked to add 2 to this number aloud, then asked to add 3 to this new number aloud, then 4 to that, then 5 and then again 2, 3, 4, 5, etc., in rotation. For instance, if the number given were 9, the consecutive sums would be: 11, 14, 18, 23, 28, 32, 37, 39, etc. Every thirty seconds E is to announce a new number with which S is to start at once a new number keep adding throughout at your maximum speed.

Taking first some column of numbers, E should offer S a trial by speaking aloud the number at the top, and should check his accuracy in the adding by following down the column. If a mistake is made call out the correct number and at the same time make a dot opposite it on the page.

For the formal experiments, E uses the columns in their order from left to right. The numbers to be announced every thirty seconds to S are the ones at the top of the columns. As S adds aloud, E follows down each column and corrects and marks errors. At the end of each thirty seconds he draws a line under the last number given by S to indicate how many numbers were added and at the same time announces aloud the new number of the next column.

One person as S is to work constantly in one single bodily position until he has been taken over twenty columns three times – a total of 30 minutes of adding time. He should be seated looking at a point on the wall and throughout his work he should not vary his bodily posture, but keep the same sitting position, both feet flat on the floor, head and arms in the same pose, etc. This is important. (*Dashiell*, 1931; *Watson*; *Robinson*; *Pillsbury*; *Gates*).

Bibliography

Agarwal, (1979). A study of interaction pattern in families in relation to decision-making. Masters Dissertation. Punjab Agricultural University, Ludhiana.

Agarwal, S.P. & Jain, R.K. (1991). Alternative Building Materials as Wood Substitute – A Comparative Study in abstracts of *National Symposium on Substitute for Wood in Buildings.* 12-13 Dec. Roorki: CBRI.

Agrawal, B.K. (1988). Classification of Engineering Materials. In Raghavan, V. (1996). *Materials Science and Engineering: A First Course.* New Delhi: Prentice Hall of India Pvt. Ltd.

Agrawal, B.K. (1988). Classification of Materials. In Raghavan, V. (1996). *Materials Science and Engineering: A First Course.* New Delhi: Prentice Hall of India Pvt. Ltd.

Agrawal, K. (1986). Status and role of middle class educated earning women in the Indian Family. Paper presented at the World Congress of Sociology. Delhi. In Sharma, P. (1993). Involvement of women in decision process in the management of farm households of hill region of UP. Doctoral Dissertation. MSU. Baroda.

Ahlstrom, R., Berglund, B., Berglund, U., & Lindvall, T. (1986). Formaldehyde odor and its interaction with the air of a sick building. *Environment International.* 12:189-295.

Ak, N.O., Cliver, D. O. & Kaspar, C.W. (1994). Cutting boards of plastic and wood contaminated experimentally with bacteria. *Journal of Food Protection.* 57: 1, 16-22.

Ak, N.O., Cliver, D. O. & Kaspar, C.W. (1994). Decontamination of plastic and wooden cutting boards for kitchen use. *Journal of Food Protection.* 57: 1, 23-30.

Allen, A. A. and *Fischer, G.J. (1978).* Ambient temperature effects on paired associate learning. *Ergonomics,* 21:95-101.

Anastasi, A. (1982). Psychological Testing (5th ed.). New York: Macmillan Publishing Co. Inc.

Andersen, I., Lundquist, G. R. & Molle, L. (1975). Indoor Air Pollution due to Chipboard used as a Construction Material. *Atmospheric Environment*, 9:1121-1127.

Annual Report. (1977). Infestation Laboratory. Report: Danish-Pest-Infestation-Laboratory. pp.92

Anonymous (1999). The Chamoli, India Earthquake of March 29. *Report of National Science Foundation.*

Ashton, H.E. (1969). Weathering of Organic Building Materials. In *Canadian Building Digest*. Canada: National Research Council Canada.

Azer, N. Z., Mc Nall, P. E. & Leung, H. C. (1972). Effects of heat stress on performance. *Ergonomics*. 15:681-691.

Bailey, J.E. & Ollis, D.F. (1986). Biochemical Engineering Fundamentals (2nd ed.). New York: McGraw Hill Book Co.

Baker, V. (2005). http//www.google-home.com

Barros, O.B. (1993). Ergonomia: O ambiente de trabalho, a productividade e a qualidade de vida em odontologia. *Sâo Paulo: Pancast*.2:385

Berglund, B., & Lindcall, T. (1986). Sensory reactions to "Sick Buildings". *Environment International*. 12:147-159.

Best, J.W. & Khan, J.V. (1980). Research in Education. Seventh Edition.

Bittencourt, M. S. (2001). Environmental Climate in the Workplace—An ergonomic approach. *Proceedings of International Congress on Humanizing Work and Work Environment*, Bombay, 11-14 December, 2001. ed IIT Bombay.

Blackman, T.; Evason, E.; Melaugh, M and Woods, R. (1989). Housing and Health: A case study of two areas of West Belfast. *Journal of Social Policy*. 1026.

Boardman, B. (1986, December). Seasonal mortality rates and cold homes. Paper presented at conference on healthy housing: A diagnosis. University of Warwick.

Bowyer, J. (1973). Guide to domestic building surveys (2nd ed.). London: The Architectural Press.

Branbech, M. & Bonnefoy, X. (2001). Housing and Health: The Eastern European Challenge. *Open House Int.* 26(2):8-22.

Brodger, R. S. (ed). (1995). Introduction to Ergonomics. New York: McGraw- Hill Inc.

Buell, W.F., Tosh, F.E., Martin, R.J. Schnurrberger, P.R. & Rose, N.J. (1973). Studies of Histoplasmosis in two Illinois communities. *Illinois Medical Journal.* 144 1: 30-33.

Burridge, R. & Ormandy, D. (1993). Unhealthy Housing: Research, Remedies and Reforms. Madras: E & EN SPON.

Byrne, D.S., Harpigson, S., Keithley, J. & McCarthy, P. (1986). Housing and Health. Gower. Aldershot.

Carlisle, A. (1976). The utilization of forest biomass and forest industry wastes for the production and conservation of energy. Ontorio: Canadian Forest Services, Canada.

Carstairs, V., & Morris, R. (1989). Deprivation and Mortality: An Alternative to Social Class. *Community Medicine.* 11:210.

Cecere, M.C., Gurtler, R.E., Chuit, R. and Cohen, J.E. (1998). Factors limiting the domestic density of Triatoma infestans in north-west Argentina: A longitudinal study. *Bulletin of the WHO,* 76: 4, 373-384.

Challa, G. (1993). Polymer Chemisrty—An Introduction. Horwood: Ellis.

Chand, N. (2003). Filled Polymer Composites— A Review. Bhopal: Regional Research Laboratory.

Christensen, C.M. (1975). Molds, mushrooms and mycotoxins. In CAB abstracts. pp. 264

Cohen, N.J. & Squire, L.R. (1980). Preserved Learning and Retention of Pattern Analyzing Skill in Amnesia: Dissociation of Knowing How and Knowing That. *Science.* 210:207-210.

Dashiell, J.F. (1931). Fundamentals of Objective Psychology. Boston: Houghton Miffin.

Dashiell, J.F. (1949). Fundamentals of General Psychology. Pitman.

Davenne, L., Daudeville, L. & Yasumura, M. (1996, August). Failure of bolted joints loaded parallel to the grain:

Experiment and simulation. Paper presented at International Council for Building Research Studies and Documentation. Bordeaux, France.

Despot, R., Trajkovic, J., Sinkovic, T. and Turkulin, H. (1999). The influence of type and colour of coat on the durability of exterior fir wood joinery. Paper presented at International Conference on Surface Properties and durability of exterior wood building components, Zagreb, Croatia.

Detroit. (1986). In Merritt, F.S. (Ed.), *Standard Handbook for Civil Engineers.* (3rd ed.). NY: McGraw Hill.

Dias, J.C.P., Dias, R.B., Pinto, D.J.C. & Borges, D.R. (1982). Housing and the Control of Vecotors of Human Chagas' disease in the state of Minas Geras, Brazil. *Bulletin of the Pan American Health Organization,* 16: 2, 117-129.

Dietz, A.G. H. (1986). Plastics for Architects and Engineers. Cambridge: The M.I.T. Press. In Merrit, F.S. (Ed.), *Standard Handbook for Civil Engineers.* (3rd ed.). NY: McGraw Hill.

Dinwoodie, J.M. (1977). Causes of deterioration of UF chipboard under cyclic humidity conditions. *Holzforschung,* 31: 2, 50-55.

Dunleavy, P. (1981). Mass housing in Britain. London: Oxford University Press.

Eichler, W., Cerny, V. & Schiffel, K. (1973). Plagues of mites (Ornithonyssus bacoti (Hirst) in a farmhouse. *Sngewandte Parasitologie.* 14: 3, 169-176.

Foster, H.D. (1992). Health, Disease and the Environment. London: Belhaven Press.

Foster, L.J.R., Foller, C.R. & Leng, R.M. (1994). Int. Sym. On Bio-product Processing. In Radhakrishna, S. and Arof, A.K. (Ed.), *Polymeric Materials.* New Delhi: Narosa Publishing House.

Fuller, T.E., Hulchanski, J.D., & Hwang, S. (2000). The housing/ health relationship: What do we know? *Rev Environ Health.* 15(1-2):109-133.

Garrett, H.E. & Woodsworth, R.S. (1979). Statistics in Psychology & Education. New York: Green and Co. In Patel, S. (1996). Assessment of micro-environmental quality of household kitchen in Baroda City. Doctoral Thesis. MSU Baroda.

Glasgow District Council. (1989). Housing Conditions Survey. Glasgow: Glasgow District Council.

Graf, E. (1989). Ecological aspects of chemical control of the house longhorn beetle. *Holz-als-Roh-und-Werkstoff,* 47:9, 383-387.

Gudkin, M. and Offord, R. (1971). A guidebook to bio-chemistry. Cambridge: University Press.

Gupta, M.L. (1981). Business Statistics. Vadodara: Shri P.N. Publishers. In Patel, S. (1996). Assessment of micro-environmental quality of household kitchen in Baroda City. Doctoral Thesis. MSU Baroda.

Harper, C. (1986). Handbook of Plastics and Elastomers. NY: McGraw Hill. In Merrit, F.S. (Ed.), *Standard Handbook for Civil Engineers.* (3rd ed.). NY: McGraw Hill.

Heinrich, J., Holscher, B. and Wjst, M. (1998). Housing and allergic sensitization in children. *Zentralblatt – fur – Hygiene – und - Umweltmedizin.* 201:3, 211-228.

Helmstadter, G.C. (1964). Principles of psychological measurement. NY: Meredinth Publishing Company.

Hunger, B. (1994). Die Bedeutung groBer Neubaugebiete in der Wohnungs und städtebanpolitik der DDR – Historischer Rückblick. *Inf Raumentwickl.* 9:595-609.

Hunt, S. M., Martin, C. & Platt, S.P. (1986, December). Health and Housing in a Deprived Area of Edinburgh. Paper presented at Conference on Unhealthy Housing. A Diagnosis. University of Warwick.

IIDA. (1990). Intro. Ergonomia: Projecto e producao. São Paulo: Edgard Blucher.

Ineichen, B. (1993). Homes and Health: How Housing and Health Interact. London: E & FN Spon.

Ineichen, B. (1993). Homes and Health: How Housing and Health interact. England: E & FN Spon.

Jain, S. & Mehta, A. K. (2003). Extruded Profiles from Wood – Plastics Composites. New Delhi: Manas Plastics Technology Consultants. In *proceedings of the POLYBUILT 2003.* Roorki: CBRI.

Johanning, E., Gareis, M., Yang, C.S., Hintikka, E.L., Nikulin, M. Jarvis, B. & Dietrich, R. (1998). Toxicity screening of materials from buildings with fungi indoor air quality problems (Stachybotrys Chartarum). *Mycotoxin Research.* 14: 2, 60-73.

Kaur, M., & Sharma, M.L. (1983). Rural women and advancing agricultural technology: A study of an Indian state. *Journal of Social and Economic Studies,* 2 (1&2): 23-25.

Keithley (1993). In Ryd, H. My home is my castle – Psychological Perspectives on "sick buildings". *Buildings Environment.* 26 (2): 87-91.

Kenjo, Toshiko. (2005). http//www.google/IFLA PAC Asia/

Khursheed, F., Parwez, M.Q., Niyogi, U.K. & Khandal, R.K. (2003). Utilization of Plastic Waste in Road Construction. Shri Ram Institute of Industrial Research. Delhi. In *Proceedings of the POLYBUILT 2003.* Roorki: CBRI.

Kirk, T.K. (1975). Ann. Rev. Phytopathological. 9:185. In Radhakrishna, S. and Arof, A.K. (Ed.), *Polymeric Materials.* New Delhi: Narosa Publishing House.

Kothari, C.R. (1990). Research Methodology: Methods & Techniques. New Delhi: Wishwa Prakashan.

Krieger, J., & Higgins, D.L. (2002). Housing and Health: Time again for public health action. *American Journal of Public Health.* 92:758-768.

Kuppuswamy, B. (1954). Elementary Experiments in Psychology. Oxford: Oxford University Press.

Lapko, A., Steckiewicz. R. & Tribillo, R. (1989). Effects of biological degradation in wood after several hundred years' use. *Ochrona Przed Korozja,* 32: 1, 6-9.

Mathews, G., Davies, D. R., Westman, S.J. & Stammers, R.B. (2000). Human Performance: Cognition, Stress and Individual Differences. Psychology Press.

Mattson, J. & Oftedal, T. (2005). Research on Bio-deterioration of Cultural Heritage in Norway. Norway: Oslo. *www.w08-oftedl.pdf*

McCarthy, P., Harrison, S., Keithley, J. & Byrne, D.S. (1985). Housing type, housing location and mental health. *Social Psychiatry.* 20: 125-130.

Merrit, F.S. (Ed.). (1986). Standard Handbook for Civil Engineers. (3rd ed.). NY: McGraw Hill.

Miral, M.S., Kumar, K. & Dumka, R.K. (2003). Traditional Construction Practices in the Seismically Active Areas of Uttaranchal. ENVIS Bulletin: *Himalayan Ecology.* 11 (1): 37.

Modern Plastic Encyclopedia. (1986). New York: Plastics Catalog Corp. In Merrit, F.S. (Ed.), *Standard Handbook for Civil Engineers.* (3rd ed.). NY: McGraw Hill.

Monroy, C., Rodas, A., Mejia, M. and Tabaru, Y. (1998). Wall plastering and paints as methods to control vectors of Chagas diseases in Guetemala. *Medical-Entomology-and-Zoology.* 49:3, 187-193.

Motohashi, K. (1996). Outdoor exposure test of pigment stain for wood. *Proceedings of IUFRO Working Party, Surfacing and Finishing of Wood.* Forest Research Institute. 9-11 Dec. Kuala Lumpur, Malaysia.

Naas, I-de-A. (1986). Agricultural structure problems in tropical countries. *Agricultural Mechanization in Asia-Africa and Latin America.* 17: 3, 67-71.

Oliveira, Filho. AM. (1997). Use of new tools for triatomine control in different entomological situations in the American Continent. *Revista-da-Sociedade-Brasileira-de-Medicina-Tropical.* 30:1, 41-46.

Ost, J. W.P., Allison, J., Vance, W.B. & Rstlc, F. (1969). A Laboratory Introduction to Psychology. USA: Academic Press.

Oxford University Press. (1994). Oxford Dictionary. Oxford: Oxford University Press.

Panday, K.K. (2003). Natural and Accelerated Weathering of Rubberwood. Banglore: Institute of Wood Science and Technology.

Pederson, B., & Gravesen, S. (1983). Allergic alveolitis precipitated by micro-organisms in the home environment. *Ugeskv. Laeger.* 145: 580-581.

Peterson, L.R., & Peterson, M.J. (1959). Short-term retention of individual verbal items. *Journal of Experimental Psychology.* 58:193-198.

Pike, L. (1981). Morbidity and Environment. In Merrit, F.S. (Ed.). (1986). *Standard Handbook for Civil Engineers.* (3rd ed.). NY: McGraw Hill.

Pires, H.H.R., Borges, E.C., Andrade, R.E., Lorosa, E.S., Diotaiuti, L. and de-Andrade R.E. (1999). Peridomicilliary Infestation with Triatoma Sordia Stal, 1859 in the country of Serra do Ramaldo, Brazil. *Memorias do instituto oswaldo cruz.* 94: 2, 147-149.

Public Health in England. (1988). In Ryd, H. (1991). My home is my castle – Psychological Perspectives on "sick buildings". *Buildings Environment.* 26 (2): 87-91.

Raghava (2003). Trends in building materials. In *Proceedings of the POLYBUILT 2003.* Roorki: CBRI.

Raghavan, V. (1996). Materials Science and Engineering: A First Course. New Delhi: Prentice Hall of India Pvt. Ltd.

Ranson, R. (1991). Healthy Housing — A Practical Guide. London: E & FN Spon.

Razek, M.M., Hanna, G.B., Salam, E.M.El and Farag, N. (1984). Computer simulation and thermal measurements of passive heated and ventilated buildings. *Proceedings of 3rd International PLEA Conference.* Maxico City. 6-11 August. 952-959.

Rosen, S.L. (1993). Fundamentalprinciples of polymeric materials. John Wiley.

Rudnai, P., Viragh, Z., Vaskobi, E. B., Zsamboki, B.M., Orban, E.E., Farkas, I. Paldy, A. Farkas, H., Karpati, Z., Takats, Z., Vegso, V.A., Sarkany, E., Varro, M., Toth, I., Skafszky, A., Harkaly, M., Sedlak, M., Cszari, D., Pazsit, C., Ujlaky, I., Acsady, L. and Horvathne, J.A. (1999). Rolc of some indoor factors in the prevalence of respiratory symptoms and allergy among school children in six towns of Hungary. *Egeszsegtudomany*. 43:3, 196-208.

Ryd, H. (1991). My home is my Castle – Psychological Perspectives on "sick buildings". *Buildings Environment*. 26 (2), 87-91.

Sastry, A.R.K., Premkumar, M.J. & Sitaramam. (2003). Coir reinforced wood composites as wood substitutes. Hyderabad: Indian Institute of Chemical Technology. In *proceedings of the POLYBUILT 2003*. Roorki: CBRI.

Sastry, C.A. & Radhakrishna, S. (1998). Biopolymers and their applications. In Radhakrishna, S. and Arof, A.K. (Ed.), *Polymeric Materials*. New Delhi: Narosa Publishing House, 197-220.

Sayer (1984). In Burrridge, R. and Ormandy, D. (1993). *Unhealthy Housing: Research, Remedies and Reforms*. Madras: E & EN SPON.

Sethi, R.M. (1983). Female labour in agriculture: A case study of Punjab. In Dak, T.M. (Ed.). *Women and Work in Indian Society*. New Delhi: Discovery Publishing House.

Sharma, P. (1993). Involvement of women in decision process in the management of farm households of hill region of UP. Doctoral Dissertation. MSU. Baroda.

Singh, B. & Gupta, M. (2003). R & D on polymeric building materials at Central Building Research Institute. CBRI. Roorki. In *proceedings of the POLYBUILT 2003*. Roorki: CBRI.

Singh, S. (1991, Dec.). Fire Gas Toxicity of Organic Building Materials. In National Symposium on substitute for wood in buildings. CBRI. Roorki.

Singh, S. (2000). Ergonomic Assessment of Modes of Carrying Load and Related Health Hazards in Women Farmers of Kumaon Hills. Masters Dissertation. G.B.Pant University of Agriculture and Technology. Pantnagar.

Smith, S. (1989). Housing and Health: A Review and Research Agenda, Discussion Paper No. 27, Glasgow University Center for Housing Research. In Burrridge, R. and

Ormandy, D. (1993). *Unhealthy Housing: Research, Remedies and Reforms*. Madras: E & EN SPON.

Sorenson, S. and Brunnstrom, G. (1995). Residential energy efficient lighting: Assessing Intervention Study among older people. *www.ncil.com.*

St. Leger, A.S. & Yarnell, J.W.G., (1977). Housing conditions, respiratory illness and lung function in children in South Wales. *British Journal of Preventive and Social Medicine.* 31,183-188.

Strachan, D. & Elton, P. (1986). Relationship between respiratory morbidity in children and the home environment. *Fam. Pract.* 3: 137-142.

Stryer, L. (1981). Biochemistry (2nd ed.). San Francisco: Freeman and Co.

Talwar, U. (1984). Social Profile of Working Women. Jodhpur: Jain Brothers Ratanga Roa.

Taylor, R. (2000). Wood Markets – The Solid Wood Products Outlook. 2000 to 2004. Vancouver: R.E. Taylor and Accociates.

Townsend, P., Davidson, N. & Whitehead, M. (1988). Inequalities in Health. Harmonsworth: Penguin.

Trajkovic, J., Despot, R., Govorcin, S. & Turkulin, H. (1999, April). Moisture content in pinewood and firwood exterior joinery. Paper presented at International Conference on surface properties and durability of exterior wood building components, Zagreb, Croatia.

Turkulin, H. & Sell, J. (2002). Durability of wooden facades. Part I: Physical and Structural Protection. *Drvna Industrija,* 53: 1, 33-48.

Turkulin, H., Jirous, R.V. and Grbac, I. (1997). Surface durability of the wooden buildings. *Sumarski List,* 121: 11-12, 617-629.

United Nations Economic Commission for Europe (UNECE). (2002). Guidelines on condominium ownership of housing for countries in transition. Switzerland: NY/ Geneva.

Vadstrup, S. (2005). Working Techniques and Repair Methods for Plaster Decorations on Facades. In Plaster Architecture Project Essay. *www.google.com*

Verma, S.K. (2003). Plastics-moulding the future of building construction industry. Chennai: Central Institute of Plastics Engineering & Technology. In *proceedings of the POLYBUILT 2003*. Roorki: CBRI.

Webb, D.J.T. (1985). Low cost housing and parasite vectors. *Parasitology Today*. 1: 2, 65-66.

Weekly Epidemiological Record. 1990. Chagas' Disease. 65: 34, 257-261

Wood Handbook. (1986). National Forest Products Laboratory. Washington D.C.: U.S. Government Printing Office. In Merrit, F.S. (Ed.), *Standard Handbook for Civil Engineers*. (3rd ed.). NY: McGraw Hill.

Woodson, W. (1981). Human Factor Design Handbook. New York: McGraw Hill.

Xavier, R., Bonnefoy SanEng, Matthias, B., Brigitte, M. S., Kubanychbek, M., & Nathalie, R. (2003). Housing and Health in Europe: Prelimenary results of a pan-european study. *American Jl. of Public Health*. 93(9), 1559.

Yang, W.B., Liu, Y.X., Li, J., Yang, W.B., Liu, Y.X. & Li, J. (2001). Advances in the research of recycled wood plastic composite. *World Forestry Research*, 14:5, 26-30.

Zigel' Boim, S.N. and Obsedshevskii, V.S. (1988). The resistance of protective/decorative coverings of fibreboards in atmospheric conditions. *Derevoobrabaty-vayushchaya-Promyshlennost*. 4: 5-7.

Index